Celebrating
TEACHERS
A VISUAL HISTORY

Celebrating TEACHERS
A VISUAL HISTORY

DR. DEIRDRE RAFTERY

BARRON'S

Conceived, edited, and designed by Fil Rouge Press Ltd., 46 Voss Street, London E2 6HP

First edition published in 2016 in the United States and Canada by Barron's Educational Series, Inc.

First published in the United Kingdom in 2016 by Fil Rouge Press Ltd.

All inquiries should be addressed to:
Barron's Educational Series, Inc.
250 Wireless Boulevard
Hauppauge, New York 11788
www.barronseduc.com

ISBN: 978-0-7641-6814-7

Library of Congress Control No. 2015952443

Printed in China by Wai Man

10 9 8 7 6 5 4 3 2 1

Publisher: Judith More
Editor: Jenny Latham
Designer: Janis Utton
Picture Researcher: Emily Hedges

Contents

Introduction

It has been a pleasure and a challenge to write this visual history of teachers, designed to celebrate the teaching profession. The pleasure derives from the opportunity to reflect on the myriad important roles that teachers have played, which are so central in social history. The challenge has been to somehow capture as much of that history as possible, within the limits of time and space.

Since antiquity, teachers have been recognized for the wisdom that they contributed to successive generations of learners. But teachers also suffered in the name of their profession. They carried enormous burdens, especially in times of war and crisis. Private employers and public policy makers, who did not value their hard work, often ignored them. While it has not been possible to capture all of the many and varied ways teachers have coped with challenges, *Celebrating Teachers* offers glimpses of the work of some extraordinary women and men whose teaching lives should never be forgotten.

The challenges and joys of the teaching profession have been represented in film, drama, and fiction, and through such work, artists have given a voice to teachers. For this reason, it was important to include literary and cinematic representations of teaching alongside historical evidence about the profession. It was also important to capture the voices of young teachers today and to show how their students value them greatly.

What emerges, then, is a book in four parts. The first part takes readers on a journey through education in ancient times, pointing to the important role of the teacher around the globe, from Rome to China, from Greece to India. The medieval period is examined, with its universities, colleges, and convents. The chapter on the early modern period reveals how the philosophy of education shaped classroom practice, and also shows how the materialities of schooling developed in different countries. The second part of the book looks at teaching in the 19th century, with particular focus on North America and Europe. The education impetus of Christian missionaries who left Europe for parts of Asia and Africa is also noted. The 19th century was a period of great change in education, widening opportunities for mass schooling and opening higher education to women. Some of the revolutions in education are captured in this part of the book.

The third part brings readers into the 20th century, and many readers will be familiar with the contexts and changes. The profound influence of war and economic depression on the teaching profession is seen, and the voices of some teachers are captured, thanks to the work of oral historians. It also looks at how popular culture portrayed teachers, and how many teachers who became writers won public acclaim for their work. Finally, in the fourth part of the book, we look at some educational innovations and innovators. The impact of technology is addressed, and teaching initiatives and projects are celebrated.

The celebratory perspective of the book, in part, reflects my own biography. I spent six years as a schoolteacher before becoming a university teacher and teacher educator. I have a high regard for the teaching profession, not least because I have had the privilege of visiting hundreds of classrooms over the past 25 years. While researching this project, I have tried to be inclusive and impartial, but it is inevitable that very many teachers and education innovators will not appear in the pages of this book. To those teachers, and to teachers everywhere, I dedicate this book in admiration and gratitude.

Dr. Deirdre Raftery, FRHistS

1 BEGINNINGS

In all cultures, parents have been traditional providers of informal education to their children, yet teachers also had a major role in passing knowledge, forming young minds, and shaping cultures. Formal teaching, where wise people instructed students in groups, dates at least from 1500 B.C. The development of teaching theories and practices and the formal training of teachers are more recent phenomena, with the rise of publications and university study of education in the late 17th century.

Ancient Times

Education has been the main instrument of change in most societies, and it has also transmitted cultural traditions and contributed to creativity, stability, and progress. The influence of educational ideas and practices in Ancient Greece and Rome reach into the present day and have shaped how we view teachers and schools. Philosophers, including Plato and Aristotle, developed theories around the right ways to educate youths and prepare them for adult life and social responsibility. Their ideas are still studied by teachers today and form building blocks for an understanding of how to be a "good teacher."

MESOPOTAMIA

The earliest known civilizations provided forms of education in temples, where moral codes were developed and humans defined ways of living in communities. Priests and wise men also determined how to regulate the calendar and engaged in astronomical observation. They had a need to write down their ideas using symbols, and the beginnings of reading and writing developed in this context.

The origin of writing: 3000-2000 B.C.

Later Mesopotamian mythology attributes the origin of writing to Nabu, the god-scribe. We know that humans engaged in forms of graphic art during the Paleolithic period, but we can only hypothesize about the precise way in which such designs became symbols with a specific meaning that teachers could transmit to their pupils. What seems to have happened is that a primitive notation system was developed, which could be scratched onto pieces of moist clay with a stylus made from wood or bone. By the turn of the third millennium, symbols of notation, together with the first nine natural numbers, were being used by Mesopotamians. A system of thousands of complex symbols was developed, which remained in use for almost 3,000 years. It is impossible to know whether or not formal public schools existed in this period, but the existence of a sophisticated system of symbolic writing strongly suggests that there was some sort of organized schooling for scribes.

Teaching and literacy: 2000-1500 B.C.

In the second millennium, writing was revered, and the priestly study of words was of great importance. The transmission of wisdom was mainly oral, but some carefully guarded secrets were written down. By the end of the second millennium, scribes became more common. There was prestige attached to becoming a scribe, as literacy indicated social superiority. Formal schooling took place in the Tablet House, or *edubba*, and excavations have revealed school exercise tablets dating from about 2500 B.C. Masters, or *dubsars*, who prepared work for the pupils, ran the Tablet Houses. The soft clay tablet was used for writing, and was then corrected and rolled back into a ball to be reused as a fresh tablet. As students became more proficient, they progressed to longer tablets with more inscriptions. Scribal literacy demanded obedience and compliance by the pupils, and did not allow for creativity.

In Ancient Egypt, hieroglyphics and a system of reckoning for the purpose of measuring and calculation were also highly valued. Rewards for ability in these areas, and for showing diligence and obedience, could include advancement in governmental administration. It was even suggested that success in scribal studies could lead to immortality, and papyrus, the writing board, and the reed pen were tools of great value. Kai, the son of the nobleman Mesehet, claimed that the memory of writers could last forever. "Be a scribe, put it in thy heart," he wrote.

on to learn a trade or craft. At the age of 14, boys from wealthy families commenced the next stage of their education, either at a school or with a philosopher. Advanced education included preparation for military life.

Spartan education differed from Athenian education. Spartan society required that all men be soldiers, and their training included the equivalent of a modern-day "boot camp," the *agoge*. Here, boys and young men learned how to become indomitable fighters. Spartan girls and women had advanced physical education and learned to run, throw the javelin, and wrestle.

The Greek philosophers and education

Considered to be the father of Western philosophy, Socrates (470/469–399 B.C.) was a classical Greek philosopher whose ideas have mainly come to us through the writings of his famous pupil, Plato (c. 427–348 B.C.). Plato was the founder of the first institution of higher education in the Western World: the Academy in the Grove of Hecademus/ Academus, outside Athens. His legacy to educational thought, and in particular to the art of teaching, is universally recognized, and he presented the earliest-known argument for the education of women equal to that of men. Through the use of dialogues, he taught about many subjects including rhetoric, mathematics, logic, ethics, and religion. The dialogues presented the thoughts of Socrates, and the style of debating and discussion in the dialogues became known as the Socratic method. This method is arguably the most important pedagogic style; it includes the use of questions to draw out critical and analytical answers, and to engage the respondent in reflective learning. The goal is insight—even today, teachers study Plato not only because of his extraordinary legacy to thought, but

Above:

Mosaic depicting Plato's Academy, the School of Athens, from Pompeii, Italy.

ANCIENT GREECE

The cultural heritage of the Mesopotamians and the Egyptians made contributions to the culture of the Greeks, Romans, Byzantines, Hebrews, and Arabs. In Athens, education commenced at home. For parents who could afford it, children went to school once they turned seven. There, they learned to write, read, and count. Physical education was also very important for Athenian boys and girls, though only boys progressed to the gymnasium to perfect their strength. Physical prowess and beauty were valued greatly.

While children of the upper ranks had a formal elementary education until the age of 14, poor children had a limited education and often went because knowledge and understanding can be best achieved via the use of debate, analysis, and logic.

ANCIENT ROME

The Roman education system was based on the Greek system, and an emphasis was placed on advanced education for sons of important Roman families. Romans who wished to study at an advanced level went to Greece to study philosophy. While Romans placed less emphasis on athletics and literary education, they viewed the military arts as very important. Like the Greeks, the Romans provided very limited education for women.

Wealthy families employed tutors to teach their sons at home, and later, some boys attended schools. The teacher was known as the *litterator*, and he used poetry and literature to educate his pupils. Later, boys would study under a *grammaticus*, who would polish the verbal and written skills of his students. The most promising students continued their studies with a *rhetor*. The study of rhetoric prepared them for political life or to study philosophy. All of these types of teachers played very important roles, not only in the transmission of knowledge, but also in supporting the social fabric. Advanced education was an elite pursuit, which conferred status and wealth. From this early point in Western culture, it is possible to discern some of the attributes of education that can still be seen in the present day: it was a passport to success and power, and a means whereby those with ability could become leaders and idealists.

CHINA

In China, the educational thinking of Confucius (551–497 A.D. approx) emphasized the importance of the teacher as a source of wisdom and good example. The student should learn the arts of music, archery, ritual, calligraphy, chariot-riding, and computation, and should also study the art of oration, good government, and morality. The connection between education and the development of morality and wisdom was clear, and Confucius used careful questioning and reflection in his own teaching to develop students' ability to reason and think. Good education should teach students how to be

humane and responsible. He wrote, "He who learns but does not think is lost. He who thinks but does not learn is in great danger." (*Lunya*, 2.15.)

INDIA

Buddhism originated in India between the 6th and 4th centuries, and spread to central and Southeast Asia, Korea, China, and Japan. Buddha (in Sanskrit, "the awakened one") was a teacher, and the "three jewels" of Buddhism are the Bhudda, *dharma* ("the doctrine"), and the *sangha* (the monastic order or community of monks). The wisdom imparted by Buddhist monks attracted pupils from around the world. The chief aim of a Buddhist education was the attainment of Nirvana through the spread of Buddhism. Finding solutions to life's problems were part of the concern of Buddhist education, and teachers used questioning, reflection, and discussion as their main teaching methods.

Above:

This illustration dating from 1814 shows a man using an early Chinese abacus. Today, abaci have an upright wood or metal frame, with sliding beads strung on wires. The earliest abaci were beans or stones moved in grooves in wood, stone, or metal trays. The Chinese abacus, known as a suanpan, *dates back to at least the 2nd century* B.C. *Ancient abaci from Mesopotamia and Rome have also been found.*

The Medieval Period

Between the fall of Rome in 476 A.D. and the beginning of the Renaissance in the 14th century, Europe lived through a period sometimes referred to as the Middle, or "Dark," Ages. The idea that Europe had entered a dark period gained currency in the Renaissance, when people looked back and decided that Europeans had squandered the educational and cultural riches of ancient Greece and Rome, and had made no significant scientific or artistic developments. However, far from being a period where education stagnated, the medieval period in Europe witnessed important developments in the education of men, women, and children.

MONASTIC SCHOOLS

The European continent, following the fall of the Roman Empire, had no single government, and during the medieval period, the Catholic Church emerged as the most powerful force. Under the direction of churchmen and women, schools and universities flourished in the European West, and teachers were much respected.

From the 4th to the 12th centuries, monastic schools attached to medieval monasteries and convents were the most important institutions of learning, and they kept the study of the classical texts alive. They transcribed important works, learned ancient Greek, translated key documents, illustrated manuscripts with beautiful calligraphy and drawings, and developed libraries that would become important repositories of knowledge.

In Italy, Benedict of Nursia (Saint Benedict) founded 12 communities of monks and devised the Rule of Saint Benedict by which Benedictine monks and nuns would live. This Rule included that nuns and monks should read and study. The influence of Benedict, who is viewed as the founder of Western monasticism, had a huge effect on the development of European civilization and culture after the detrimental effects of the fall of the Roman Empire.

Many other monastic centers of learning were founded in countries including Spain, France, and Ireland. At the Spanish monastery of Saints Cosmas and Damian near Toledo, the students were taught scientific subjects such as medicine and the rudiments of astronomy. Irish monastic schools were known all over Europe, receiving students from Rome, Britain, Germany, and even Egypt to study the classics, literature, science, and religion. The Irish monasteries also sent scholars abroad to spread learning. Many of the young men who studied with the monks were the sons of chiefs, kings, and noblemen, and were destined for military and civil life. Monastic schools also made a contribution to wider society by allowing pilgrims and travelers to stay at the monasteries.

MEDIEVAL CONVENTS

In medieval female monasteries, nuns provided education for novices who were going to become nuns. Many of these convents also provided schooling for daughters of wealthy families, and in some cases, the nuns also taught young boys. Commissioners who visited Saint Mary's convent in Winchester, England, in 1536 found that all of the pupils were the children of lords, knights, and gentlemen. While the extent of convent schooling for the laity in the Middle Ages is not clear, probably about two-thirds of all convents in Britain gave some tuition

Opposite:

Parents offering money to secure their child education at a monastic school. Miniature from Decretum Gratiani, *12th century.*

Above:

Héloïse and Abélard, illustration on vellum from Le Roman de la Rose, *by Jean de Meung (c. 1370).*

in return for fees. French female monasteries also educated lay people. At the abbeys in Argenteuil and Angers, for example, girls and women received a classical education from the nuns.

Although female monasteries were cloistered, and the occupants were therefore cut off from the wider world, there is clear evidence that their studies had an impact on society. For example, one medieval nun, the Abbess Hildegard of Bingen (1098–1179), made important contributions to natural science and healing. In many cases, the education that nuns possessed had been gained before they entered the convent. These women were perfectly placed to educate other nuns and members of the laity. They were also suited to leadership roles and positions of power within the Church. Noblemen who wanted their daughters to be abbesses in important monasteries would make sure their daughters had a very good education.

Héloïse d'Argenteuil (c.1095–1164) and Pierre Abélard (1079–1142)

The famous French Abbess Héloïse, who conducted an intellectual dialogue in letters with Pierre Abélard, was educated at the abbey at Argenteuil, near Paris. Little is known of her youth, but she was a ward of her uncle, the Canon Fulbert, who had placed her in the convent to be raised by the nuns. Brilliant at Hebrew, Latin, and Greek, she was famous throughout Europe for her learning.

By the time she was about 27, her ability made her suitable to become a pupil of Pierre Abélard, a popular teacher and philosopher, in Paris. His eventual seduction of Héloïse resulted in her becoming pregnant. While the couple married secretly, he contrived to place her in the convent at Argenteuil where she had been raised, so that he could continue his profession as a philosopher. At his encouragement, she became a nun and eventually rose to the position of Abbess. Abélard became a monk at the Abbey of Saint Denis in Paris. Héloïse and Abélard carried out a correspondence in Latin, some of which has survived. In one letter, her formidable intellect is clear as she lays out 42 problems of scriptural interpretation for his consideration. While the story of Héloïse and Abélard is subject to scholarly disagreement, this medieval romance between a pupil and her teacher has inspired poets such as Christina Rossetti and Alexander Pope. It is referenced in many novels and has influenced painters, composers, dramatists, and filmmakers.

Hildegard of Bingen (1098–1179)

A Benedictine nun, Hildegard was a mystic, a writer, and a philosopher. Her education was received at Disibodenberg, a Benedictine convent in the Palatine forest (now part of Germany), where she was sent at the age of eight. Like Héloïse d'Argenteuil, Hildegard would eventually become prioress of the convent that she had attended. She later moved her nuns to a convent in Bingen.

"... an authentic teacher of theology and a profound scholar of natural science and music."

Pope Benedict XVI

Describing Hildegard of Bingen in his address at St. Peter's Square, Rome, May 2012

Hildegard was skilled at healing and wrote treatises on natural science that displayed her knowledge of herbal and chemical remedies. She was also a poet, musician, and noted rhetorician.

Although women at that time were not allowed to teach and preach in public, Hildegard made four preaching tours throughout Germany. She left a vast amount of written work, much of which was published and well regarded in her lifetime. Although Hildegard has not been canonized a saint, Pope Benedict XVI honored her by making her a Doctor of the Church in 2012. This is a title that has been conferred on only 35 other people, all of whom are saints of the Catholic Church, and only three of these doctors are women.

Above:

Hildegard receives a vision in the presence of her secretary, Volmar, and her confidante, Richardis, c. 1220–30.

Above:

Aquatint portrait of Margaret Beaufort, Countess of Richmond and Derby (1443–1509), founder of St. John's College Cambridge and mother of Henry VII of England. From The History of Cambridge, *published in 1815.*

and at York (627 A.D.). Many cathedral schools still operate today, including Salisbury Cathedral School (1091 A.D.), where the choristers of Salisbury cathedral are educated.

Although the cathedral schools initially functioned to prepare boys for religious life, they soon attracted pupils who wanted to study Latin and other subjects that would prepare them to pursue professions such as law and medicine. Famous teachers attracted pupils from all over Europe, who would travel great distances in order to study under the direction of great masters such as Gerbert of Aurillac, founder of the cathedral school at Rheims, who made the school famous for the teaching of science. Another renowned teacher was Pierre Abélard (see page 18), of one of the cathedral schools of Paris, who taught theology and philosophy.

Although the cathedral schools had emerged within a context of traditional Latin learning, they provided a very wide range of teaching. Pupils were taught by teachers whose expertise varied from law and medicine to the different elements of the seven liberal arts: the *quadrivium* of science subjects (astronomy, geometry, arithmetic, and music), and the *trivium* of grammar, rhetoric, and logic.

THE MEDIEVAL UNIVERSITY

The word *university* is derived from the Latin phrase *universitas magistrorum et scholarium*, or "community of teachers and scholars." Medieval European universities were established in Italy, Spain, France, Portugal, and England. These universities derived from the older monastic schools and cathedral schools, and their primary purpose was to provide education for clergymen. As the medieval university, or *Studium Genaerale*, developed, it did not confine itself to receiving only the local population. Rather, it welcomed students from everywhere and provided learning in theology, law, and medicine in addition to the arts. Teaching was usually carried out by lecturers who were holders of master's degrees.

Universities with considerable status included the University of Salerno, Spain, where the world's first

CATHEDRAL SCHOOLS

In medieval Europe, cathedral clergy ran schools attached to their cathedrals, where the boys of noble families could receive an education. Often these boys were being prepared for the church, and cathedral schools provided a kind of apprenticeship training. Cathedral schools also educated choral scholars to provide church music.

In Britain, among the oldest and most famous cathedral schools were those at Canterbury (597 A.D.), school of medicine was founded in the 9th century. There, both women and men taught the students. One of the most famous women academics of the 12th century was Trota of Salerno, a physician and medical writer whose text *De curis mulierum* ("On Treatments for Women") was famous in many parts of Europe.

The University of Paris, widely known as the Sorbonne, had begun in the middle of the 12th century, but was formally founded by the Catholic Church in the first year of the 13th century. Regulations concerning who could teach at the Sorbonne were introduced in 1215 by the Apostolic legate Robert de Courçon. To teach the arts, a candidate had to be at least 21 and should have studied for at least six years. To hold a chair in theology, the academic had to be 30 years of age, with eight years of theological studies. Importantly, university teachers had to have good morals.

SCHOOLING IN JAPAN

In Japan between the 6th and 9th centuries, education ideas traveled from China. Buddhism and the ideas of Confucius played a role in the development of education traditions, and by the 9th century, there were several institutions of higher learning in what is now Kyoto. Japanese education was also influenced by the arrival of Christian missionaries, such as the Society of Jesus (Jesuits). Francis Xavier and a group of Jesuit fathers arrived in Japan in the 1540s, and other Christian missionaries such as the Dominicans and the Franciscans followed. The Jesuits tried to influence rulers rather than preaching and teaching directly to the commoners, and in this way, they tried to avoid suspicion while still teaching the Catholic faith. When Christianity was repressed, teaching fell to "hidden Christians," who passed on the rituals and prayers, usually from father to son.

Right:

Jewish teacher and pupil, illustration on vellum, from the Coburg Pentateuch *by Simhah ben Samuel Halevi, 1395.*

The Early Modern Period (c.1450–1800)

The most important development of the modern period was the invention of moveable type printing. It is considered to have laid the basis for the modern knowledge-based economy by facilitating the spread of learning in an unprecedented fashion. A German printer and publisher Johannes Gutenberg (1398–1468) invented a system whereby pieces of type were individually cast in a mold, which allowed them to be reproduced endlessly. When the type was set and inked, it was possible to print large amounts of text in uniform "fonts." The speed and clarity that this introduced into the whole process of producing pamphlets and books had a remarkable impact on the teaching and the spread of both general information and specialist knowledge.

Right:
Woodcut of a master with four pupils. Title page to a Latin schoolbook Incunabulum *by Johannes Synthin, 1498.*

THE IMPACT OF THE PRINTING PRESS

The printing press was crucial to the spread of the ideas of the Renaissance, the Reformation, the Enlightenment, and the Scientific Revolution. While the printing press that Gutenberg presented to the world did not have the kind of technological operating systems of a modern-day computer, it brought about a step-change in human communication, perhaps only comparable to the impact of the Internet in modern times. Without a doubt, its contribution to the education of teachers was incalculable, as we can see from the large volume of works that appeared on every aspect of teaching and learning.

Right:
Gutenberg inventing the printing press; oil painting, c.1830, by Jean-Antoine Laurent. Johannes Gutenberg's invention changed the way in which pedagogues could spread learning and theories of education.

PHILOSOPHIES OF EDUCATION

Between the 7th and the 15th centuries, several books of formal instruction appeared in the English language. These were useful to parents who wanted to instruct their children correctly at home, and to teachers who needed guidance on the appropriate education for boys and girls. During the Renaissance, a distinct genre of "conduct literature" appeared, which provided instructions on the religious education and the correct behavior of children. Protestant religious reformers, such as Thomas Becon (1512–67) and Miles Coverdale (1488–1569), stressed that mothers should have a good knowledge of the Bible so they could instruct their children and secure their salvation.

Catholic humanist scholars also wrote extensively about education. In *The Education of a Christian Prince* (1516), Dutch teacher and theologian Desiderius Erasmus (1466–1536) not only drew on the classical texts to instruct the reader, but also argued that a good teacher should have a gentle disposition and excellent morals. In 1540, he wrote a very popular instruction book, translated as *A Handbook of Good Manners for Children*, teaching youths how to behave in various situations. Other prominent thinkers who wrote about teaching include the Catalan education theorist Juan Luis Vives and the Czech pedagogue John Amos Comenius.

Juan Luis Vives (1493–1540)

Educated at the Estudio General, Valencia, and at several colleges in Paris, Vives eventually settled in Bruges and was introduced to Erasmus, by whom he was greatly influenced. In the 1520s, he visited England, where he knew Sir Thomas More, and he became tutor to Mary, daughter of Henry VIII and Catherine of Aragon. In 1524, Vives' book, *The Education of a Christian Woman*, appeared. In it, he argued that while women should be taught, they should not become teachers.

Vives argued that women should study the Bible, the church fathers, and Christian poets. However, because women neither governed nor taught, they did not need to study grammar, logic, or history. He wrote that the goal of their education should be "the

study of wisdome, which doth enstruct their maners and enfourme their lyving, and teacheth them the waye of good and holy lyfe."

Vives believed that fathers should direct the teaching of their daughters, and that husbands should determine what their wives should be taught. In a book called *The Office and Dutie of an Husband*, he argued that husbands should limit their wives' education, and that silence was the greatest female virtue. "Let not thy wife be overmuch eloquent, nor full of her short and quick arguments, nor have knowledge of all histories, nor understand many things, which are written," Vives instructed.

John Amos Comenius (1592–1670)

Many educationists consider Comenius, who was born in Nvince, Moravia, in the area that is now in the Czech Republic, to be the father of pedagogy. By articulating education theories, he brought a rigor to the study of education that positioned it beside other academic disciplines. This approach is most evident in his best-known education work *The Great Didactic*, which he completed in 1631 and published a few years later. His writings on education theory would reach into the 19th century and continue to influence teachers and education theorists.

Comenius believed that education was a lifelong process, and that teachers should strive to make it enjoyable. He argued that teachers should pay attention to the ages of their pupils, making learning more practical and pleasant. He opposed the kind of pedantic teaching that obliged pupils to learn facts by rote and, instead, favored using examples from nature and from ordinary life. He believed that students of European culture needed to study Latin firstly, as it "unlocked" many languages, and works of literature and art. His book *The Gate of Tongues Unlocked* (1632) had a huge impact on the teaching of Latin and other languages. There is evidence that Comenius was asked to consider becoming the first president of Harvard University, but he declined the offer.

Jean-Jacques Rousseau (1712–78)

Born in Geneva, Rousseau was one of the most influential education philosophers of his era, and indeed, his influence on teachers continues to this day. His work is read not only by education students, but also by scholars interested in political philosophy and the ideas of the French Revolution.

Rousseau was deeply interested in human nature, how humans develop morality, perfect a sense of imagination and a sense of self. His major treatise on education was *Émile, or On Education* (1762). In it, he explored how human goodness can be developed and how the ideal citizen should be educated. The book is divided into five sections, three of which concern the education of a young boy called Émile, while the fourth section is concerned with the education of adolescents.

Rousseau had an original conception of the "teacher," believing that children have three teachers: nature, things, and mankind. The education given to the young Émile should prepare him emotionally, physically, and intellectually. It should include developing his sense of reason, so he can consider moral issues and make decisions in adult life. Rousseau believed that teachers should not oblige children to learn things by rote or to memorize information that had no relevance to the experience of childhood. Teachers who taught "facts" and regulated the behavior of their pupils were merely "training" the children and keeping parents satisfied. Teachers should allow "Nature" to instruct; they should let children explore, discover, and create. Such processes, he believed, were central to real education.

In the fifth section of *Émile*, Rousseau wrote about the kind of education appropriate for Sophie, the ideal female companion or wife for Émile. His views on female education caused controversy and were the subject of much debate. He stated that women should be passive and weak, and their education should prepare them to please men. One of Rousseau's critics was teacher and writer Mary Wollstonecraft, who argued that female and male education should be the same in an equally controversial publication *A Vindication of the Rights of Woman* (1792).

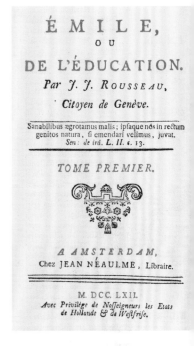

Above:

Title page of Émile *by Jean-Jacques Rousseau, published 1762.*

"*Young teacher, I am setting before you a difficult task, the art of controlling without precepts, and doing everything without doing anything at all. This art … is not calculated to display your talents nor to make your value known to your scholar's parents; but it is the only road to success.*"

Jean-Jacques Rousseau

From Émile *(1762)*

Above:

Sir Thomas More and his family, oil on canvas (1592), by Rowland Lockley after Hans Holbein the Younger's 1527 original (destroyed by fire in the 18th century).

WOMEN AND LEARNING

While the common view was that girls did not need a classical education since they would not play a role in public life, Sir Thomas More (1478–1535) provided his young wife with an education in music and literature, and raised his daughters in an atmosphere of learning. They were given the same classical education as his son and provided an example to other noble families of how daughters should be educated. Erasmus (see page 24), having seen how accomplished More's daughters were, was influenced in his thinking about how girls should be taught.

Anna van Schurman (1607–78)

The earliest record of a woman entering debates about female education is a book by the brilliant Dutch scholar Anna Maria van Schurman, which first appeared in 1641, and was translated from Latin into English as *The Learned Maid, or Whether a Maid may be a Scholar* (1659). Educated at home in her native Cologne, Anna van Schurman was an exceptional linguist and a pious Protestant. She was flawless in Persian, Arabic, French, English, Latin, and Italian, and it is, therefore, perhaps unsurprising to find that she thought all women should be allowed to have an academic education. She argued that women should be allowed to study traditionally "male" subjects including grammar, logic, rhetoric, metaphysics, and history. But she did not suggest that women should use this education to compete with men in the public arena; rather, their education should make them happy and virtuous Christians. Learning, she argued, would make women better able to contemplate and understand the love of God.

"In every town, village and even hamlet, there are persons found who take upon themselves the great and important charge of female education: and over their doors are seen in letters of gold, A Boarding School for Young Ladies. "

Clara Reeve

From Plans of Education *(1792)*

Mary Astell (1666–1731)

In England, an early champion of female education was Mary Astell, who was born in Newcastle-Upon-Tyne to a family who provided her with a good home education. Her interest in girls' education influenced her to write a book that became widely known and controversial. Titled *A Serious Proposal to the Ladies for the Advancement of their True and Greatest Interest* (1679), the book presented an argument that the vanity and foolishness displayed by many young ladies was a result of their shallow education.

She was deeply critical of the kind of education given to middle and upper class girls, which consisted mainly of training in the "accomplishments" of music, drawing, dancing, and singing. Astell proposed that the female "vices" of pride and vanity could be erased if young women were well educated and learned how to make sound judgments. Those who opposed academic education for women and girls criticized this radical idea, but it gained currency with other circles of intellectual women such as the famous "Bluestockings."

The "Bluestocking" Circle

In the 18th century, a group of educated English women and men lead by the society hostess Lady Elizabeth Montagu (1720–1800) became known for their literary salons and their writing on many aspects of education. The circle included Hester Chapone (1727–1801), who wrote *Letters on the Improvement of the Mind, Addressed to a Young Lady* (1773), and Elizabeth Carter (1717–1806), who produced a translation of *Sir Isaac Newton's Philosophy Explain'd for the Use of the Ladies* (1739).

Many books and magazines appeared for use at home to educate young ladies. These included *An Introduction to Botany* (1760), *The Female Preceptor* (1813–14), *The Female Instructor* (1815), and *The Female Spectator*, which appeared monthly from 1744–46. The opinion-forming magazines for ladies had a genteel tone and were sometimes to be found in academies and boarding schools for girls. Though boarding schools were becoming more widespread, teaching standards in these schools was uneven, and in some cases, the teachers were themselves poorly educated. Some schools were speculative ventures, set up by people who simply wanted to make money by pandering to the demands of parents. In 1792, Clara Reeve wrote in *Plans of Education* that boarding schools were not being run by teachers, but by "adventurers of all kinds."

Left:
Portrait of Anna Maria van Schurman by Jan Lievens (1607–74).

A PERSPECTIVE VIEW OF THE FOUNDLING HOSPITAL, WITH EMBLEMATIC FIGURES.

Above:

A 1749 engraving of the Foundling Hospital, Camden, London, showing mothers with babies waiting outside the gates.

Opposite:

Portrait of philanthropist Captain Thomas Coram by William Hogarth, 1740.

TEACHING THE POOR

Although much 18th-century writing about teaching focused on the middle and upper ranks, there were also many individuals and groups who were concerned about the education and care of poor children. In orphanages and foundling homes, they provided shelter and some instruction for children. Religious groups managed some of these institutions. Both Catholic clergy (nuns, priests, and brothers) and Protestant voluntary societies were involved in providing residential and non-residential care and teaching. Foundling homes in Germany were established as early as the 12th century, where the Brothers of the Holy Spirit founded nine homes in Germany by 1198. By the end of the 17th century, there was an orphanage in every German city with a population greater than 10,000. In Spain, most foundling homes were founded in the 16th century, in places such as Seville, Madrid, and Salamanca. In Ireland, the Hibernian Marine Society (1766) provided education and apprenticeship training for orphans and the children of seamen. In France, the *Hôpitaux Généraux*, or general hospitals, run by the French Catholic Church cared for orphans and vagrants. In Italy, children were taken into institutions such as the *Ospedale della Pietà* in Venice, where some were taught music and singing.

Thomas Coram (1668–1741)

An English sea captain, Thomas Coram was born in Lyme Regis, Dorset; he went to sea before he was 12, and spent much time in the American colonies. He founded a shipbuilding business in Massachusetts in 1694 and was a successful businessman, later returning to England to continue his business interests. His greatest, and most lasting, achievement was building the London Foundling Hospital between 1741–45.

At that time, the term "hospital" was used to refer to care institutions, including residential children's homes that had schools attached. The London Foundling Hospital was founded to provide education and care for deserted children. It attracted the support of the painter William Hogarth who became a governor of the home and designed the uniform worn by the children. The composer George Frederick Handel was also a Foundling Hospital governor, and he had a benefit performance of his great work *Messiah* performed there. Handel also donated a score of the famous oratorio to the Foundling Hospital. The hospital had some success in the teaching of music, and many of its pupils went on to play in army and navy bands.

The home was relocated to Hertfordshire in 1935. In the 1950s, institutional care for orphaned children was phased out, and adoption and fostering became the acceptable form of care. The home ceased most of its functions, and a charity called The Thomas Coram Foundation for Children was established. While the original buildings no longer stand, some of the site remains and is known as Coram's Fields. There is a museum there that illustrates the history of childhood at the Foundling Hospital and remembers the names of those who lived there. In 2000, the home was the setting for the novel *Coram Boy* by Jamilla Gavin. It was adapted for the stage and played in London and on Broadway.

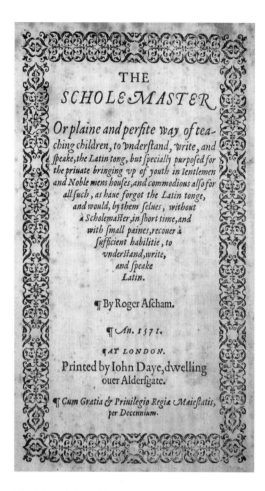

THE SCHOLEMASTER

Or plaine and perfite way of teaching children, to vnderstand, write, and speake, the Latin tong, but specially purposed for the priuate bringing vp of youth in Ientlemen and Noble mens houses, and commodious also for all such, as haue forgot the Latin tonge, and would, by them selues, without a Scholemaster, in short time, and with small paines, recouer a sufficient habilitie, to vnderstand, write, and speake Latin.

¶ By Roger Ascham.

¶ *An.* 1571.

¶ AT LONDON.
Printed by Iohn Daye, dwelling ouer Aldersgate.

¶ *Cum Gratia & Priuilegio Regiæ Maiestatis, per Decennium.*

THE SCHOOLMASTER

While medieval education was strongly connected to the Roman Catholic Church, the changes that took place in England in the reigns of Henry VII and Edward VI had a significant impact on education. The medieval universities had to submit to the supremacy of the Crown, and the monasteries were dissolved. At the great English cathedrals, the monks were replaced by secular canons, and schools were reconstituted as "King's Schools." At the universities, the properties were taken over by the Colleges, and throughout the Tudor period a process of establishing new Protestant colleges continued. For example, at Cambridge, a Benedictine hostel was refounded as Magdalene College in 1542; Emmanuel College was established on the site of a Dominican friary in 1584, and in 1596, Sidney Sussex College was established at a former Franciscan friary. Similarly, in Scotland the property of the Greyfriars was used to establish Marischal College, Aberdeen.

Most of the schools that had been attached to monasteries were disbanded, and their lands were vested in the Crown. Some endowed schools continued to operate, and under the reign of Edward VI, a number of grammar schools and guild schools were established. The grammar schools offered a classical training and included instruction in the catechism and in social skills such as deportment and gentlemanly behavior. The *English Bible* was introduced into schools, along with *Lily's Grammar* (1540) and *The King's Primer* (1545). The expansion of grammar schooling continued during the reign of Elizabeth I and the reigns of the two Stuart kings. Some privately founded grammar schools also appeared, such as Rugby (1567), Harrow (1571), and Charterhouse (1611).

With the dissolution of the monasteries and the spread of the grammar schools, Protestant schoolmasters assumed responsibility for teaching. Many regard this as the period when the profession of "schoolmastering" emerged. Full-time schoolmasters, assisted by ushers, ran the schools. They had to be men of good standing with an aptitude for teaching. There was a shift from oral methods of teaching to written methods; teachers were provided with textbooks and prepared exercises for the schoolmaster to check. The "paper book," a forerunner of the school copybook, was widely used for exercises and for translating Latin texts. At grammar schools, much time was spent teaching Latin. The teachers prepared the boys in both written and oral work, and the oral training included the use of disputations, whereby the boys engaged in competitions with each other. The climax of the oral work was the "oration" and the "declamation," and successful pupils were awarded prizes. Written Latin work included learning to write Latin sentences translated from English, and then went on to adapting classical phrases in "epistles." There was a strong emphasis on preparing the boys for university entrance, so schoolmasters had to demonstrate excellence in the classics.

Roger Ascham (1515–68)

Several writers addressed the role and duties of schoolmasters in popular publications in the 16th and 17th centuries. One of the most famous of these publications was *The Scholemaster* (1570) written by Roger Ascham and published posthumously. Ascham was born near York and educated by tutors at home. At the age of 15, he was sent to St. John's College, Cambridge. In 1537, he was appointed to St. John's College as a reader, or professor, in Greek. During his lifetime, he served as Greek tutor to Princess Elizabeth and Latin secretary to both Queen Mary and Queen Elizabeth I. He considered Elizabeth to be an excellent pupil and highly competent in languages. In *The Scholemaster*, he offered a simple method for teaching Latin, together with ideas on the ideal education for moral and intellectual development.

THE WRITING MASTER

In the Elizabethan and early Stuart period, another type of teacher that appeared was the professional writing master. Some of these men taught privately, while others worked in writing and cyphering schools. Although the most famous writing school was at Christ's Hospital, a school for orphans, writing was mainly taught to the middle and upper ranks. Writing masters often taught the children of the gentry and aristocracy in their own homes. In addition to writing, they taught history, geography, and languages. Some families paid for the services of a dancing master and a singing master in addition to a tutor for sons and a governess for daughters.

Private writing masters also ran small schools, and these usually attracted the middle classes. In addition to teaching boys to read and write, they often taught arithmetic. Some masters made additional income by publishing textbooks and manuals of instruction. The art of fine penmanship demonstrated both artistry and good education, and the elaborate scripts that survive in 17th-century manuscripts remind us of the skill attached to teaching children to write beautifully.

Martin Billingsley (1591–1662)

A leading writing master of his time, Billingsley worked in early 17th-century London and it is thought he was a tutor to Prince Charles, later King Charles I. One of his books, *The Pens Excellencie, or The Secretaries Delight* (1618), demonstrates the range of different "hands" in which people could learn to write. He offered six examples, including a style "usually taught to women" and a style he described as "the usual hand of England." Billingsley was scornful of many other writing masters, dismissing them as "a world of squirting teachers."

Above:

Seventeenth-century engraving by Michael Burghers showing Roger Ascham with Princess (afterward Queen) Elizabeth I.

Above:

An original copy of The New England Primer, *1690.*

and many scrambled an education together under the direction of a clergyman or at a "dame school." These were small private enterprises where women taught the "three Rs" in their own homes or cabins. Teachers usually had only a handful of books to work from, and teaching supplies were scant. Pupils learned their lessons by rote, and classroom discipline was often harsh. Simple textbooks with rhyming couplets, such as *The New England Primer* (1690), wove religious instruction and simple reading exercises together, and reminded children that "The idle fool is whipped at school."

In some New England states, girls were educated similarly to boys, and they were, therefore, eventually able to take up teaching positions. Indeed, by the early 19th century, women teachers had replaced schoolmasters in many Boston schools.

Quaker Teachers

Quakers promoted female education and recognized the important role that educated women had in poor relief and in ministry. In Philadelphia, there were some very well-regarded Quaker schools. The earliest of these was founded in 1689 at the encouragement of William Penn. Today, William Penn Charter School is an independent private school ranked as one of the top schools for sending its pupils to Harvard, Princeton, and Yale. The Quaker commitment to education in the late 17th and early 18th centuries resulted in about 40 schools being founded in Pennsylvania, and a further 20 in New Jersey by 1750.

Quakers became vocal in the abolition movement by the second half of the 18th century, and teachers played an important role in instructing others about equality. A celebrated martyr to the abolitionist cause was the Quaker teacher Richard Dillingham from Peru Township (now Morrow County, Ohio). Imprisoned for aiding the liberation of three slaves, he died in the Tennessee State Penitentiary in 1850.

The New Orleans Ursulines

An order of teaching Sisters, or nuns, the Ursulines were the founders of the oldest girls' school, and the oldest continually operating Catholic school, in the

TEACHERS IN THE NEW WORLD

Institutional learning in the "New World" of North America began to slowly spread in the early 17th century following the arrival of settlers from different religious groups, including the Quakers, Puritans, and Anabaptists. The early colonists prioritized the building of schools along with houses of worship. The importance of schooling in the salvation of souls was recognized by various denominations, and they valued the teachers that they placed in positions of responsibility running their schools. The Puritans, who began the Plymouth colony in 1620, believed that schooling should be harnessed in support of the spread of their values. Schoolmasters provided religious instruction as well as academic education in a disciplined atmosphere. Their responsibilities included transmitting Puritan culture and teaching their pupils self-control and a strong work ethic. Schools usually had only one room, and children of all ages were taught together.

In Massachusetts Bay, as religious and political communities grew in the 1630s, education was provided for children from the age of eight. The first public school, Boston Latin School, was founded in 1635 to cater to Boston's elite. But schooling was not only the preserve of the wealthy. There were also schools for the children of merchants, ministers, and settlers. Not all children had access to a school,

United States: the Ursuline Academy, New Orleans. The Ursuline order was founded in Italy in 1535 for the care of the sick and the education of girls, and their patron saint is Saint Ursula. They first came to New Orleans in 1727, though some members of the order had founded a convent school for girls in Quebec as early as 1639. The Quebec school taught both Native American village girls and French girls. The program of learning included reading, writing, prayers, and "Christian habits." While the Ursulines were initially sent to French colonies, they quickly spread to other regions and founded schools and colleges in many other areas including Boston (1820), Brown County, Ohio (1845), Cleveland (1850), New York (1855), Louisville (1858), and Chatham, Ontario (1860). The order also expanded considerably in Europe.

The group of 12 Sisters who arrived in New Orleans in 1727 had survived a difficult journey from Europe. Dressed in heavy black serge habits, they learned to cope with the damp Louisiana nights, the mosquito bites that made their faces swell, and the torrential rains. Once established, they provided schooling for both French girls and enslaved girls. From the outset in both Quebec and New Orleans, the Ursulines showed a commitment to inclusion. Among the lists of "firsts" attributed to the Ursulines in the United States is the provision of academic education for free women of color (a group also known as Creoles of color), for Native Americans, and for female slaves until abolition. The Ursulines also played an important role in health care and health education. They opened the first hospital in New Orleans and the first social welfare center in the Mississippi Valley.

As teachers, the Ursuline Sisters showed great commitment to scholarly education, and they established colleges for women such as Ursuline College in Ohio (1871), the College of New Rochelle (1904), and Brescia College (now University) in 1919. Other Ursuline college foundations in the United States included Mount St. Joseph College in Kentucky (1925) and the Great Falls Junior College for Women in Montana (1932), which is now the University of Great Falls. The Sisters also founded what is now the oldest school in Dallas: the Ursuline Academy of Dallas. In 1893, they founded the Ursuline Academy at Wilmington, Delaware. Ursuline schools were also founded in California, St. Louis, and Springfield, Illinois.

Left:

Charcoal drawing depicting the landing of the first Ursuline nuns in New Orleans, 1727, by Marie-Madeleine Hachard, a novice who accompanied the 12 original nuns who journeyed there.

Above:

Statue of John Harvard in Harvard University yard.

NEW WORLD UNIVERSITIES

A year after the founding of Boston Latin School, Harvard University was founded (1636). The distinguished Massachusetts institution was named after its first benefactor, John Harvard, who left his library and half of his estate to the fledgling university in 1638. Over a period of almost 380 years, many future American presidents graduated from Harvard University, including John Adams (1755), Franklin D. Roosevelt (1903), John F. Kennedy (1940), and Barack Obama (1991).

While Harvard is the oldest American institution of higher education, several other substantial colleges were founded in the American colonies, before the United States became a sovereign nation. In Virginia,

William and Mary College was founded in 1693. Other prestigious institutions of higher education followed, including Yale University (1701), the University of Pennsylvania (1740), and Princeton University (1746). The other "colonial colleges" are Columbia (1754), Brown (1764), Rutgers (1766), and Dartmouth (1769). Both Dartmouth College and the University of Pennsylvania developed from initiatives in secondary schooling. Dartmouth's founder, Eleazar Wheelock, established Moor's Charity School in 1754. In 1768, Dartmouth began operating as a collegiate department of the school. In Pennsylvania, the statesman Benjamin Franklin brought about the establishment of the Academy of Philadelphia, which added its institute of higher education in 1755.

Noah Webster and the "Blue-backed Speller"

With the founding of the first universities, there were new opportunities for learning. Young men who were educated at the colonial colleges were able to make a contribution to raising the standard of teaching. Many became clergymen and teachers, who taught at schools or privately, and prepared boys for university entrance. One such educated clergyman was the Reverend Nathan Perkins, a Congregational minister who had attended Princeton. Perkins tutored the young Noah Webster (of *Webster's Dictionary*) to enter Yale in 1774.

Webster studied law and later became a teacher in Hartford, Connecticut. He abhorred the imported English schoolbooks that were the staple fare of 18th-century American schoolchildren and wanted a book that would teach the words that were in common use in America. Webster wrote and published *A Grammatical Institute of the English Language* (1783), which became known as the "Blue-backed Speller" because of its distinctive cover. Although Webster was one of the founders of Amherst College (1812), he is perhaps best known for his work as a lexicographer. His dictionaries were widely used, and the "Blue-backed Speller" was the most popular American book of its time. It was the staple item in every teacher's armor, and had sold about 60 million copies by the end of the 19th century.

Above:

Noah Webster (1758– 1843) developed the famous blue-backed spelling book and dictionary.

Academic Dress

While the cartoon caricature of the teacher dressed in a black gown and mortarboard is a familiar one, the cap and gown was a medieval invention. Academic robes originated in the 12th and 13th centuries. Most scholars at that time were clerics and wore clerical garb under plain gowns. The elaborate robes and colored silk hoods seen at graduations today have their origins in the medieval practice in which scholars dressed in highly embellished clothes like those of cardinals or bishops when awarded degrees.

The more utilitarian black robe worn by teachers as recently as the 1960s had practical purposes: it kept the wearer warm, and it provided a kind of uniform for schools that wanted to abolish "excessive" dress. In classrooms, the wearing of a gown meant that teachers were easily distinguished from their students. Well into the 20th century, schoolteachers threw on their gowns when going to class in order to avoid ruining their clothing with the dust from chalkboards.

While European academic dress varies very significantly from university to university, academic dress in the United States has been standardized to a considerable degree. American colleges favor closed robes, while the robe is usually worn open in Europe. The colors and shapes of the gowns and hoods indicate the different universities, the different degrees, and the status of the wearers. Today, in most schools, teachers' dress code is "smart casual,"

and the day of the mortarboard is over. However, most new teachers are advised to wear appropriate dress to work. In order to avoid confusion around what constitutes appropriate clothing, many schools have introduced dress codes for teachers.

The academic cap, or mortarboard, that is worn with academic gowns probably developed from the *biretta* worn by Roman Catholic clergymen. Fifteenth-century Italian noblemen also wore caps with a flattened top, which indicated their military and civil power. In the 16th and 17th centuries, university graduates who held a master's degree wore a cornered cap. It is said that the academic cap became known as a mortarboard because of its similarity to the hawk tool used by plasterers when working with mortar. In 1950, two American inventors patented a mortarboard design that is widely used today, adding fiberglass into the manufacture of its top to make it sturdy.

From left to right:

American graduates in purple gowns with black mortarboards; Princess Mako of Japan graduates in the black cap and gown worn at the International Christian University, Tokyo; the doctoral robe of the University of Nigeria is worn with a red mortarboard; an international student on his year abroad in Germany wears a black gown with a sash in the colors of the German flag.

Left:

The Rev. William Guinon Rutherford, Headmaster of Westminster School. The academic gown and mortarboard was regular dress for 19th-century schoolmasters in English private schools. Spy cartoon from Vanity Fair, 1898.

Above:

The schoolmaster in black cap and gown, as seen here in the movie Goodbye Mr. Chips (1939), was a feature of British classrooms until the mid-20th century.

Below:

College presidents Charles Eliot of Harvard and Arthur Hadley of Yale walking in a graduation procession with other professors at Columbia College, New York, 1903.

2 THE NINETEENTH CENTURY

In the 19th century, the training of teachers became more formal, and the teaching profession witnessed many changes. Ideas about teaching traveled from country to country, and there was great growth in publications for, and about, teachers. The century saw significant change in pedagogic theories, as educationists were influenced by new disciplines such as psychology and anthropology.

Teachers and Charitable Education

At the start of the 19th century, elementary schooling in many countries relied on the support of charitable societies, mostly religious in foundation, and the efforts of voluntary groups. Support for establishing mass literacy grew in both Britain and the United States, in part because of religious enthusiasm and in part as a response to growing industrial development. In British colonies, Protestant missionaries ran schools. At the same time, Catholic missionaries moved all over the globe, founding schools and colleges. The charitable impulse, combined with the need to "save souls," resulted in the rapid expansion of schools and a huge growth in the teaching profession in many countries.

CHARITY SCHOOLS

In England, the Church of England was responsible for the provision of much of the available education, until the establishment of free state education at the end of the century. Education provision for the poor came from a wide array of societies, such as the Society for the Promotion of Christian Knowledge (SPCK) and the Sunday school movement. Parishes also contributed to the founding of "Bluecoat" schools, or charity schools, where children learned enough to prepare them for trade. The distinctive blue jackets worn by the pupils gave the schools their name. Charity schools and Sunday schools also existed in Scotland, Wales, and the United States in the early 19th century.

EDUCATION AND SOCIAL CONTROL

Many English writers in the 18th and early 19th centuries were concerned that teaching the poor would upset the social order. In a rapidly industrializing nation with widespread poverty and unrest, those who opposed the education of the poor feared it would add to discontent by giving the laboring classes "ideas above their station." For some, their response reflected a conservative reaction to the effects of the French Revolution. One such writer who had a great interest in education was Hannah More (1745–1833). More was a very popular writer in her lifetime, and she also founded Sunday schools in Cheddar, England. One of her most widely read publications, *Strictures on the Modern System of Female Education* (1799), made an argument for providing girls with a solid education to prepare them for motherhood and for their role in providing a moral influence in society. Between 1795–97, More published a series called *Cheap Repository Tracts*. These were moral stories designed to appeal to the general reader, which were reproduced in school reading books. They served to reinforce the social order as divinely ordained and necessary.

The popularity of the *Tracts* made it clear to many evangelicals that publishing for children could be used to teach lessons on morality and social order. Sarah Trimmer (1741–1810) also wrote tales for children that reinforced the social order. One tale reproduced in schoolbooks taught children "that it is God who makes some to be poor and some to be rich; [and] the rich have many troubles which we know nothing of, and … the poor if they are but good, may be very happy."

THE SOCIETY FOR THE PROMOTION OF CHRISTIAN KNOWLEDGE

One society that invested in educational publishing for children in Victorian England was the Society

for the Promotion of Christian Knowledge (SPCK), which had been founded as early as 1698. The SPCK founded many charity schools and produced the pamphlets and books widely used by teachers. It aimed to counter the effect of Catholic missionaries and teachers and sent its publications all over the world to British colonies where it also supported building schools and training colleges. In Ireland, it drew up schemes for converting Catholics by teaching children the defects of Catholic doctrine. In 1799, the Religious Tract Society (RTS) was founded by some of the evangelicals who were also involved in the London Mission Society (1795) and the British and Foreign Bible Society (1804). The little books produced by the RTS would become part of the staple reading fare in schools and in thousands of Sunday schools.

SUNDAY SCHOOL TEACHERS IN ENGLAND

While there were some Sunday schools operating in England in the 18th century, the start of the Sunday school movement is associated with Robert Raikes (1736–1811). He founded a Sunday school for

Above:

A writing lesson at Christ's Hospital School, Horsham.

Above:

1878 print showing mission teachers D.L. Moody and J.V. Farwell with a group of 14 boys at their first Sunday school class, North Market Hall, Chicago. The boys' "street names" are listed by number. Only No. 1 "Red Eye" (standing far left) and No. 7 "Madden the Butcher" (sitting with broom far right) are numbered; those sitting on the ground in the front row must represent Nos. 8–14.

children from the slums of Gloucester, where scripture was taught and the Bible was used to teach reading and writing. By 1831, approximately 1.2 million children were attending Sunday schools in England. At a time when children were used for labor from an early age, Sundays were the only "free" days on which schooling could be offered to the poor. The use of amateur teachers drawn from the congregations meant that the pupil-teacher ratio was good, with about 12 pupils to every three amateur teachers in Anglican Sunday schools in 1851. However, the disadvantage of relying on untrained teachers was that the standard of teaching was very uneven. In 1841, one of the officials carrying out inquiries for the Children's Employment Commission stated that the teachers had little

understanding of education or of how to communicate knowledge to children, and many were unfit to teach. The role of the Sunday school in England changed once the state national school system was developed, and its purpose no longer included the provision of literacy.

AMERICAN SUNDAY SCHOOL TEACHERS

In the United States, the 19th-century Sunday school was an idea adopted from England in the 1790s. Industrialists set some of them up to educate the children of their factory workers. Others were established by religious activists in large cities such as Philadelphia. Many African-Americans received their limited education in Sunday schools at this time. In New York City, African-Americans made up nearly 25 percent of the pupils at schools run by the City Sunday School Union Society. By the middle of the 19th century, with the spread of public schooling, Sunday schools no longer taught literacy and concentrated on their evangelical mission. The inclusive nature of Sunday schools meant that different ethnic groups were instructed together. For example, First Nation people and whites were instructed at the Sunday school in Oklahoma Indian Territory in 1909.

Socialist Sunday schools were also popular in the late 19th and early 20th centuries. They were established to provide an alternative to the Catholic and Protestant Sunday schools and to teach the ideals of socialism to children. The first was founded in New York in 1880 by the Socialist Labor Party of America, and other Socialist Sunday schools were founded in working-class areas in Chicago and Philadelphia.

In 1874, the Chautauqua Institution was founded in New York as a teaching camp for Sunday school teachers. However, many American Sunday school teachers, like those in other countries, were selected from the congregation on the basis of their good character and knowledge of the Bible.

Today, many Sunday schools (or Sabbath schools) continue to provide faith education, with teaching provided by lay volunteers, Catholic priests, and Protestant pastors. Two well-known Baptist Sunday school teachers are the novelist John Grisham and former President Jimmy Carter. Schoolteachers and children can get insight into the education provided by Sunday school teachers in the past by looking at the digital collection of American Sunday school books and teaching resources at Michigan State University (see page 185).

JEWISH SUNDAY SCHOOLS

Jewish education recognized the position of both the rabbi and the parent in providing faith education. However, in the United States in the 19th century, the "Jewish Sunday school" movement grew in response to the need to provide education to children—often those descended from European immigrants—who lacked a grounding in Jewish traditions and history.

Prominent in the Jewish Sunday school movement was Rebecca Gratz (1781–1869), the daughter of Michael Gratz, who had immigrated to America from German-speaking Silesia in 1752. He was descended from a long line of well-regarded rabbis. The family interest in education influenced Rebecca, who was instrumental in founding the Philadelphia Orphan Asylum, the Hebrew Education Society of Philadelphia, and the Female Association for the Relief of Women and Children in Reduced Circumstances. Gratz also established the Hebrew Sunday School, developing its curriculum and serving as its president, and was a founding member of the Female Hebrew Benevolent Society. After her death in 1869, her brother Hyman honored the memory of his sister by founding Gratz College in Philadelphia for the education of teachers.

Below:

Jewish schoolboys in Samarkand under instruction by their rebbe, or teacher. A color photograph by Russian photographer Sergei Mikhailovich Prokudin-Gorskii (1863–1944), who traveled around the Russian Empire between 1909 and 1915 using a new color photography process to capture a traditional way of life about to be lost in the Russian Revolution.

Teacher Education in the United States

Like the Sunday schools, ordinary day schools relied on "amateur" teachers to offer education to children in the 18th and early 19th centuries. Though school boards tried to oversee what was taught, the curriculum was not standardized, and teachers relied on whatever books they had on hand. Schoolhouses usually had only one classroom, and children of all ages were taught together. Attendance was often poor, and in the Southern states, schooling was not provided for enslaved blacks.

With the introduction of state "normal schools" in the 1820s, the standard of teacher education improved. These were high schools that taught pupils to become teachers, and they usually used model classrooms where student teachers could practice giving lessons. Many normal schools evolved into universities, such as Salem Normal School (1854), now Salem State University, and Winona State Normal School (1858), now Winona State University.

Samuel Read Hall (1795–1877)

In 1823, the first public normal school founded to train American teachers was established in Concord, Vermont, by Samuel Read Hall. Read Hall was a minister and a schoolteacher who was appointed principal of an academy in Fitchburg, Massachusetts, in 1822. A year later, he founded his training school for teachers, and in 1829, he helped to found the American Institution of Instruction. From 1830, he headed the English Academy and Teachers' Seminary, which was part of St. Philip's Academy in Andover. He later had leadership roles at other teacher-training academies.

A practical educator, he is credited with having invented the school chalkboard or blackboard, a cardboard version of which he used as early as 1812. At the pioneering normal school in Concord, his "blackboard" was created by painting a wall with black paint. Samuel Read Hall wrote several books for teachers including *Lectures to Female Teachers on School Keeping* (1829) and *Lectures to School Masters on Teaching* (1833).

SAMUEL READ HALL

Right:
Samuel Read Hall, father of American teacher training.

Left:
Watercolor painting entitled Blackboard *by Winslow Homer (1877). The marks on the chalkboard are a method of drawing instruction popular in American schools of the time, in which young children were taught to draw by first forming simple combinations of lines.*

Monitorial Systems

The first monitorial system was developed in England by Joseph Lancaster for instructing large numbers of pupils in his London school. The principle behind such systems was that those pupils who knew a little would help to teach those who knew less. The teacher in a monitorial school trained a group of older pupils who had mastered reading and writing to become monitors. These monitors worked with small groups of younger pupils, rehearsing their lessons and reinforcing new knowledge. Monitorial systems took hold in several countries in the early 19th century before the work of new educational theorists like Mann, Pestalozzi, and Froebel (see pages 66, 70, and 72) overturned them in the mid-19th century.

JOSEPH LANCASTER (1778–1838) AND THE MONITORIAL SYSTEM

Quaker schoolteacher Joseph Lancaster's system became popular throughout Europe because it was efficient, providing support for understaffed schools while also training young people to become teachers. Several hundred pupils could be accommodated in one classroom.

The success of the system pivoted on the teacher having good discipline and clear routines, so pupils knew where they should be, and what they should be doing. Lancaster demonstrated that a teacher was also a school "manager," and his ideas were influential not only in England, but also overseas. He traveled extensively in England, giving lectures and helping to form new schools. He also founded schools in the United States and in Venezuela, although his ventures overseas were less successful than his English initiatives.

Lancaster's teaching methods were outlined in his publication *Improvements in Education* (1803). In 1808, the British and Foreign Schools Society was formed to promote his methods. While his ideas were hugely influential, the system he promoted relied heavily on memory work and rote learning by groups of pupils, and there was little room for imagination. The schoolroom, packed with children who were being filled with "facts," was almost like a factory. Charles Dickens, in his novel *Hard Times* (1854), was critical of the way in which such Victorian schools destroyed children's creativity and individualism.

Right:

Engraving portraying Joseph Lancaster (1778–1838), an English Quaker schoolteacher who developed the monitorial system of teaching that spread to Europe and America in the first part of the 19th century

ANDREW BELL AND THE "MADRAS SYSTEM"

Born in Scotland in 1753, Andrew Bell studied natural philosophy and mathematics at the University of St. Andrews. He graduated in 1774 and set sail for America. He settled in Virginia, where he worked as a private tutor until 1781. Returning to Scotland, he trained to become a priest in the Church of England.

In 1787, Bell once again left Scotland, this time setting sail for India. He settled in Madras, becoming chaplain to several British regiments. Bell also taught—in 1789, he was appointed superintendent of the Madras Male Orphan Asylum, an orphanage for the children of deceased officers.

Bell observed children teaching each other by drawing in the sand. Impressed by how well they paid attention to each other, Bell decided to develop a teaching method whereby children with some knowledge taught those who knew less. His system,

which became known as the "Madras System," was refined at the same time as his contemporary Joseph Lancaster was developing the monitorial system in England. Like Lancaster, Bell believed that teachers should use little rewards and praise to motivate children, and he opposed the use of corporal punishment in schools.

Bell left India in 1796, returning to England, where he published *An Experiment in Education* (1797) and began to introduce his system into schools. Lancaster and Bell disputed the originality of each others' work, and both claimed to have invented the monitorial system.

The ideas of both men were eventually abandoned from the mid-19th century as teachers were drawn to the ideas of the great European educators such as Johann Pestalozzi (see page 70), Freidrich Froebel (see page 72), and Maria Montessori (see page 94), and those of the American Horace Mann (see page 66).

Above:

Color engraving entitled "Ecole D'Enseignement Mutuelle," depicting a 19th-century monitorial classroom in France. The monitorial system was introduced into France in 1815.

Teachers in Ireland

In Ireland, schooling was a contested issue from as early as the Tudor period. Successive monarchs considered that schools should be used to spread loyalty to the crown and the Protestant faith among the Irish Catholic population. Laws were enacted that forbade Catholics from running Catholic schools or from sending their children overseas to get a Catholic education. Any Catholic teacher who was found running a school was severely punished, and many were deported to Barbados.

THE HEDGE SCHOOLMASTER

The native response to the enforcement of Protestant schooling was that the Irish developed an illegal system of schools known as "hedge schools." These were speculative ventures, where teachers ran small schools in barns, outbuildings, and sometimes on the sunny side of a ditch or a hedge. Pupils paid their teachers with eggs, turf for the fire, or a few pennies. Many of the teachers were erudite Catholic scholars, and some had been preparing for the priesthood. They taught Latin, Greek, geometry, algebra, history, and mathematics. They also taught practical skills such as land measurement, and—most importantly—they taught reading and writing in the English language. This would prove useful to the many Irish people who emigrated to England, Australia, and the United States in search of work.

Hedge school teachers served other purposes in addition to teaching. They were often the local scribe, writing letters for those who could not write. They read legal documents for those who could not read, and they translated English into Irish for monoglot Irish speakers. They were also a source of entertainment, and their displays of erudition made them popular. They were skilled at reciting verse, telling stories, and they held verbal contests with other masters to display their knowledge. By 1824, there were about 9,000 private "pay" schools in Ireland, most of which were illegal hedge schools.

THE KILDARE PLACE SOCIETY: INNOVATIONS IN TEACHER TRAINING

In 1811, a group of professionals and businessmen formed a society for the education of the poor known as the Kildare Place Society (KPS). It established new primary (elementary) schools and existing "pay" schools to become affiliated with the KPS, and it published textbooks for use in schools. The KPS adopted Lancaster's monitorial system (see page 46), and developed a teacher-training college and model school. This innovation introduced practices and systems that continue to this day. Teachers were trained to manage their classrooms efficiently, take a daily roll, and reward pupils for good work.

Training for teachers took place at the KPS Model School, which opened in 1819. The school had two large classrooms and accommodation for the student teachers. Training was completed over six weeks, during which time students were not allowed to socialize or waste time. Teachers were taught how to train and work with monitors, and how to control classrooms that could contain several hundred pupils. Though teachers in KPS schools sometimes punished pupils, they were encouraged to use praise and rewards to motivate, very much in line with the ideas of Joseph Lancaster. Small prizes were supplied to schools by the KPS, and a ticket system enabled pupils to earn tickets for good work that could then be exchanged for a prize. The prizes were practical: items for needlework or a book, and constituted a very attractive reward.

Opposite:
Painting entitled The Schoolmaster's Moment of Leisure *(c. 1888) by Howard Helmick.*

Female Education

During the 19th century, the education of women evolved from private governesses teaching "accomplishments" to the daughters of the wealthy, with little or no education available to the poor, to the founding of the first seminaries for female teachers (see page 80) and, toward the end of the century, the first few degree-granting colleges for women at prestigious universities (see page 82). The majority provision of formal schooling for both girls and boys moved from the church or private individuals to the state, and in some countries or states, laws were passed making schooling for children of both sexes compulsory, raising literacy rates, and expanding the access to education for girls of all classes.

Below:

Actresses Josephine Serre and Charlotte Gainsbourg in a scene from the movie Jane Eyre, *circa 1996.*

THE GOVERNESS

Probably the most famous governess in fiction is to be found in Charlotte Brontë's *Jane Eyre*. Jane, who is described as "plain, poor and disconnected," survives her lonely education as an orphan at Lowood School and finds work as a governess at Thornfield Hall. Jane ends up marrying her employer, the brooding Mr. Rochester, as the novel reaches its happy conclusion. Other novels, such as William Thackeray's *Vanity Fair,* also had a governess as the heroine. Governesses were also the subject of paintings, such as the sentimental, though very lovely, oil by Richard Redgrave entitled *The Governess* (see opposite page). In reality, life for the Victorian governess was less romantic, and many ended up in poverty.

Governessing became acceptable as a profession for upper middle class women by the middle of the 19th century. At that time, Britain experienced a phenomenon known as "surplus women"—that is, more women than men of marriageable age in the population—as men left for the colonies or to join the army, while others felt the economic impact of the Napoleonic wars and decided to delay marriage. The changing economic fortunes of many families meant that many women could no longer expect to be supported, firstly by their fathers and then by

their husbands. However, their education—which typically included music, drawing, dancing, and French—had prepared them for very little other than a life of leisure. The only "genteel" work available to them was teaching, and many became either governesses or teachers in small private schools.

Some governesses lodged with their employer's family, while others were "day governesses." They usually taught girls from the age of six to 16, and younger boys before they left for boarding school. Governesses taught the "accomplishments" that they knew—reading, writing, playing the piano, sketching, and a little French. Those who had excel-

lent social contacts and a very good education could expect to work for the aristocracy, although they sometimes vied with continental governesses for positions. French and German governesses were seen to be quite a status symbol in any home. Middle class families keen to display their increasing gentility often hired governesses—and often fired them with little notice. Governesses were lampooned in *Punch* magazine and often ridiculed by unsympathetic writers.

Wanted, a Governess, on Handsome Terms
During the first half of the 19th century, the demand for governesses continued. As the market became

Above:

The Governess *by Richard Redgrave, RA, 1844. Governesses were the subject of paintings, such as this sentimental, though very lovely, oil. Dressed in a drab black frock, the governess sits alone with her books while her colorfully attired pupils enjoy sunshine and leisure.*

Right:

Anna H. Leonowens, ex-governess to the King of Siam's children, who inspired the musical and film The King and I. *Photograph by Wm. Notman & Son, Montreal, Canada, 1910.*

overstocked with governesses, the newspapers carried advertisements indicating the increasing demands of employers:

"Governess—a comfortable home, but without salary, is offered to any lady wishing for a situation as governess in a gentleman's family residing in the country, to instruct two little girls in music, drawing, and English; thorough knowledge of the French language is required."
The Times, June 1845

Many governesses found themselves unemployed and impoverished by middle age, and some died in the Poor House.

The Governesses' Benevolent Institution

In recognition of the plight of these "distressed gentlewomen," the Governesses' Benevolent Institution (GBI) was established in 1843 in London. Providing an employment register and training courses for governesses, the GBI relied on the support of sympathetic sponsors such as Charles Dickens. It provided lectures for young women at Queen's College, London, allowing them to pass examinations and get certification. The GBI also opened a Governesses' Home, where governesses could lodge temporarily for a small fee. The GBI brought public attention to the harsh treatment of

Anna H. Leonowens, ex-governess to the King of Siam's children, who inspired the musical and film The King and I. *Photograph by Wm. Notman & Son, Montreal, Canada, 1910.*

governesses by employers, and the reports of the Governesses' Benevolent Institution give an indication of the hardships that women teachers faced at the time.

Anna Leonowens (1831–1915)

Possibly the most famous of all Victorian governesses is Anna Leonowens, whose life inspired both Hollywood filmmakers and Broadway theater impresarios. Born in India in 1831, Anna was raised there until she married Thomas Leon Owens in 1849. They raised a small family in Malaysia, but Anna was widowed in 1859, and then tried to support herself by running a small school in Singapore. In 1862, she was recommended to King Mongkut of Siam (Thailand) as a suitable governess for the royal family. The king had 67 children by many wives. Anna Leonowens taught at the court for five

Below:

Engraving depicting The Governesses' Benevolent Institution, London, England.

GOVERNESSES' BENEVOLENT INSTITUTION.

years, before moving to the United States, where she ran a school for a while.

During her time at the Siamese court, Anna kept a journal that she later published as a successful book, *The English Governess at the Siamese Court*. The book inspired both the novel *Anna and the King of Siam* (1944) and the lavish Rogers and Hammerstein Broadway musical *The King and I*. The show was subsequently made into a very successful musical film starring Deborah Kerr as Mrs. Leonowens.

More recently, Jodie Foster played Anna in another film drama about this famous governess. The plot of the play and the two films are essentially the same: a British governess causes a Siamese monarch to reevaluate his views on slavery and sexual equality. Against a backdrop that includes the threat of English colonialism, the king struggles to protect the ancient traditions of his country while also embracing change. Anna, in addition to teaching his children their lessons, also teaches him about romantic love and freedom.

Above:

Deborah Kerr in the role of governess Anna Leonowens, in the film The King and I *(1956).*

Teachers and Mission

The 19th century saw huge growth in the Christian missionary movement. Protestant and Roman Catholic missionary teachers traversed the globe, founding and working in schools. While their main aim was the spread of Christianity, they also had a mission to educate. Some missionaries sought to convert non-Christians, while others provided schooling for Christian emigrants. Protestant and Catholic schools often vied for pupils, and their teachers believed that schools could play an important role in the "salvation of souls."

CATHOLIC TEACHING SISTERS

In Europe, the United States, Australia, and Canada, a very large part of the teaching force in the 19th century were Catholic women religious groups, typically known as nuns or Sisters by those whom they taught. They belonged to religious congregations that had a specific mission to provide education at convent and industrial schools and reformatories. In every country where they worked at that time, they relieved the national or state governments from some of the costs attached to supplying school teachers because most of them worked for free or for minimal wages. In addition, they usually built and paid for their own convents and school buildings, undertook fundraising for their educational projects, and those who were paid used their salaries to support the teaching communities. Many religious orders of nuns gave gifts of convents and school property to countries where they worked.

Nuns were part of the Catholic Church's workforce committed to spreading the faith. Education was central to that effort. In Europe, many Catholic orders were founded in the 19th century, such as the Ursulines (OU), the Loreto Sisters (IBVM), the Presentation Sisters (PBVM), the Mercy Sisters (SM), the Sisters of the Good Shepherd (RGS), and the Society of the Sacred Heart, or *Religeuses du Sacré Cœur de Jésus* (RSCJ). The Ursulines originated in Italy, while Ireland produced the Presentations and the Mercys and was home to the first Loreto convent school. The Sacred Heart order and the Good Shepherd order originated in France, as did many other orders of teaching nuns. In Australia, Mother Mary McKillop (1842–1909) founded a teaching congregation dedicated to the poor known as the Sisters of St. Joseph of the Sacred Heart (1886).

These orders spread rapidly to the New World to provide education for Catholics in the United States, Canada, and Australia, and to influence non-Catholics who might then convert to that faith. They

Below:
Pupils at Loretto Abbey, Toronto, 1909.

also were missionary nuns teaching in India, South-east Asia, and many parts of Africa. Their missionary journeys were often very arduous and included traveling for months by ship, carriage, train—and even camel and elephant. Dressed in heavy habits and wearing long veils—even in the tropics—they were a distinctive sight wherever they went.

CONVENT EDUCATION AROUND THE GLOBE

The intrepid Loreto Sisters, first established by Mother Teresa Ball in Ireland in 1821, sent young women to teach in many countries. As early as 1841, they sent a group to India. They were the first female teaching congregation to come to India, and their first school was opened in Calcutta (now Kolkata). They continued to open schools in India, particularly to teach the poor. The Loreto order also founded colleges, such as Loreto College in Calcutta, which was affiliated to the university for teacher training. Many lasting Loreto foundations were made, including convent schools at Darjeeling (1847), Lucknow (1872), Asanol (1877), and Simla (1899). Another congregation of Catholic nuns that taught in 19th-century India is the Presentation order. They sent four Sisters from Ireland to Madras in 1842, and in 1896, their mission spread to the Punjab.

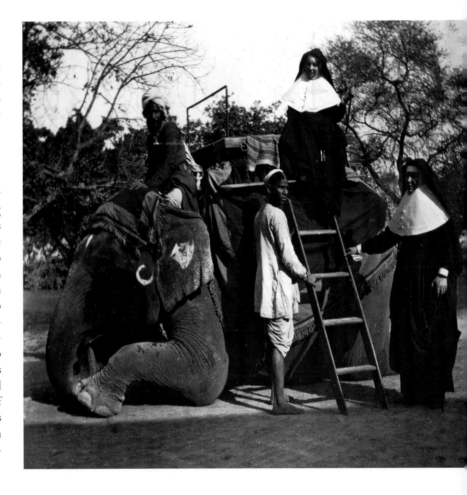

"… one of the sails … has been carried away … the cabins seem to turn upside down … waves are dashing up over the windows … darkening the room …. I got in between a bed and a trunk on the floor of our cabin [to commence] my letters home [and] every now and then a great heave of the vessel would turn things upside down … During these little interruptions it was necessary to seize the ink bottle in one hand and hold on to the bed or the trunk with the other …"

Mother Gonzaga Barry, IBVM

July 7, 1875, diary of her pioneering journey from Ireland to Australia, where she founded many schools.

Above:

Mosaic depicting French-born nun Sister Rose Phillipine Duchesne (1769–1852), with native American pupils. Mosaic set in the dome of the Cathedral Basilica of St. Louis, MO, and dating from the early 20th century.

In 1847, another group of Irish Loreto Sisters left Dublin to found a convent and school in Toronto, Canada. Under the direction of Mother Teresa Dease, many further schools were founded in Ontario, including a convent at Niagara Falls that became a scenic stopping point for European aristocrats during their travels.

In 1878, yet another Irish Loreto, Mother Gonzaga Barry, brought a group of Sisters from Ireland to Australia to found a convent school in Ballarat. The popularity of the nuns' teaching, together with their high education standards, meant that they were in demand in other parts of Australia, and they opened many schools and colleges including foundations in Brisbane, Perth, Adelaide, and Melbourne.

CONVENT EDUCATION IN THE UNITED STATES

Between 1790 and 1920, 119 European orders of nuns established foundations in the United States, and 38 American orders were founded. Their numbers spread like wildfire. In 1822, there were 200

nuns in the States; by 1920, that number had grown to 88,773. While some worked in healthcare, most were teachers.

One of the largest and most influential orders was the Society of the Sacred Heart (RSCJ, see page 54), which originated in France. Founded by Madeleine Sophie Barat in 1800, the RSCJ sent nuns to North America, New Zealand, Australia, South America, Central America, and Japan. In the United States, Sacred Heart schools kept many of the order's European traditions and French was the language of the convent. The RSCJ opened its first American foundation in St. Charles, Missouri, in 1818. Under the leadership of Mother Superior Philippine Duchesne, the order expanded to Louisiana (1821) and St. Louis (1827). Mother Philippine had a particular interest in educating Native Americans and founded a school for the Potawatomi at Sugar Creek. Although the Mother Superior didn't speak English, she was ably supported by Anna Shannon, a young nun who spoke French and English and had great leadership skills.

The RSCJ also founded schools and academies for girls in New York City (1841), Philadelphia (1847), Buffalo (1849), Detroit (1851), Albany (1852), Chicago (1858), Bryn Mawr (1865), Cincinnati (1869), Providence (1872), Boston (1880), Omaha (1881), San Francisco (1887), and Seattle (1907). Catering mainly to the middle and upper classes, they set the gold standard for convent education. The Sisters taught Christian doctrine, reading, writing, mathematics, history, music, and French. Instrumental music, painting, and singing were also important. These "extras" were a source of income for the convents. For example, school fees at St. Xavier's Sacred Heart Academy, Chicago, were $300 per year in 1877. Piano lessons cost an extra $60, and harp lessons were $80 per year. To evaluate the pupils, the Sisters used oral, written, and public examinations. At St. Xavier's, daily classroom performance was recorded, and there were competitions every Friday. On Mondays, results were read aloud. Once a month, oral examinations were conducted before the whole school. In this way, a good convent education fostered competition, high standards, and academic excellence. The pupils were taught how to write and edit school newspapers, sports were also important, and tennis became a craze.

Pupils of Sacred Heart convents are known as "children" of the Sacred Heart, and past pupils form a network that stretches around the globe. The College of the Sacred Heart in Manhattan (1881) is the oldest private school for girls in New York. This 19th-century foundation has a long list of well-known alumna, including contemporary celebrities such as Lady Gaga and Paris Hilton. It is also the alma mater of the extended Kennedy family—Rose Fitzgerald Kennedy, Jean Kennedy Smith, Eunice Shriver Kennedy, Ethel Skakel Kennedy, and Caroline Kennedy were all taught by Sacred Heart Sister teachers.

Another order that has made a huge contribution to teaching is the Congregation of the Sisters of St. Joseph (CSJ). Originally founded in France in 1650, the order was suppressed during the Revolution and refounded in 1807. In 1834, the Bishop of St. Louis, Missouri, invited the congregation to send Sisters to America. In 1836, a group traveled from France to open a school in the former French colonial town of Cahokia. There, they taught French and Creole children. They also opened a school at Carondolet, and established St. Joseph's Institute for the Deaf in St. Louis. The order quickly expanded, opening schools in Minnesota (1851), New York (1854), Pennsylvania (1860), Florida (1866), Massachusetts (1873), Michigan (1889), and Indiana (1888). Right into the 20th century, the Sisters of St. Joseph ran hundreds of schools in North America. The very large congregation was organized into several provinces, and other orders merged with it. The Sisters continue to play an important role in female education today, and are also committed to social justice issues. One of the better-known is Sister Helen Prejean of CSJ's ministry to prisoners on death row. Susan Sarandon won an Oscar for her portrayal of Sister Helen in the movie *Dead Man Walking* (1995).

"Give only good example to the children; never correct them when out of humor or impatient. We must win them by an appeal to their piety and to their hearts. Soften your reprimands with kind words; encourage and reward them. That is, in short, our way of educating."

St. Madeleine Sophie Barat

Founder of the Society of the Sacred Heart

Above:

An 1840s' engraving by J. Cochran of the Rev. James Legge, missionary teacher and scholar, with students at the London Missionary Society's Theological seminary in Hong Kong.

MISSIONARY TEACHERS IN ASIA AND AFRICA

The 19th century was known as the "great century" of evangelical revival. There was a new flowering of the spirit of evangelicalism in countries where Protestant churches already existed. Additionally, many Protestant organizations supported missionaries who evangelized in Asia and parts of Africa. As early as 1807, thousands of Protestant missionaries left Britain for China, where they established schools, hospitals, and printing presses to produce missionary publications. Missionary societies continued to grow during the century, in India, China, and Africa. In 1865, J. Hudson Taylor (1832–1905) established the China Inland Mission. Other prominent missionary groups included the London Missionary Society and the American Board of Commissioners for Foreign Missions. From the outset, missionary societies recognized the importance of schooling to the success of their projects. However, many missionary schools struggled to attract pupils. For example, in China families were wary about sending their children to Christian schools.

Male missionaries usually worked as either ministers or teachers, though some fulfilled both roles. For example, the English Methodist Rev. Samuel Evans Rowe (1834–97) had a distinguished career as a churchman while also making a contribution to teaching. He founded a school for girls in South Africa, and was chairman of Maritzburg Girls' Collegiate School in Pietermaritzburg in addition to being elected president of the Cape Town Methodist Conference, the church's governing body, in 1890.

Before the early 20th century, most Protestant missionary teachers were men. However, women were also attracted to missionary life, even though custom made it difficult for them to travel and work without a chaperone. Some women became teachers in order to assist their husbands who were ministers. Others managed to embark on missionary life alone. Methodist women from the United States, for example, played a large role in missionary education activity. Many missionary teachers found conditions difficult; it took stamina to learn new languages and to become accustomed to new ways. Missionary teachers also found the extreme climates challenging, and many suffered ill health. There was a significantly higher mortality rate among the children of missionary couples compared to those who remained at home. Unsurprisingly, many missionaries either died in the field or gave up and left for home.

There were also challenges for those who were taught by the missionaries. In Africa, Christianity created divisions within many families, as converts rejected traditional beliefs in ancestors, witchcraft, and traditional gods. Further divisions were created

Below:

The Rev. Mr. Moffat preaching to the Becona, from South African Sketches.

Above:
Lovedale Missionary Institute's Village School, South Africa.

Right:
Canadian-born George McCall Theal, teacher at Lovedale Missionary Institute, South Africa.

when converts to different Christian churches came into conflict. Despite the intentions of missionary teachers to do what they perceived was good, missionary schools and colleges contributed to social divisions and were implicated in creating a Western-educated elite.

However, some elite mission schools tried to promote racial and sexual equality, and challenge traditional boundaries. One such school was Lovedale Missionary Institute (now Lovedale Public College) in South Africa. When it was established in 1841, it provided education to Africans and white Europeans of both sexes. The school gave technical and classical instruction, and eventually developed a teacher-training college. In 1955, Lovedale passed to the state through the Bantu Education Act of 1952. Distinguished past pupils include Steve Biko.

George McCall Theal (1837–1919)
Born in Canada, George McCall Theal has been widely acknowledged for his contributions to teaching, history, and archives in South Africa.

Theal emigrated to South Africa as a young man and became a teacher, working in several public schools before being appointed to a teaching post in 1875 at Lovedale Missionary Institute. There, he taught English, geography, and bible studies, and was in charge of the monthly publication the *Kaffir Express* (later *Christian Express*), produced in both English and Xhosa. He became an expert on Bantu and published extensively.

Mary Ann Aldersey (1797–1868)

While Catholic nuns were missionary teachers in the late 17th century, single Protestant and Dissenting women first entered the mission field in the 19th century. One of the first unmarried British women missionary teachers was Mary Ann Aldersey. Born in London, England, she had the opportunity to study Chinese there under the prominent missionary leader Robert Morrison. In 1837, she went to Indonesia to found a school for immigrant Chinese girls in Batavia (present-day Jakarta). In 1843, she opened another girls' school in Ningbo in China. Though she was not formally attached to any missionary society, she employed the daughters of English missionaries to work with her as teachers. In 1861, she handed her school over to the Church Mission Society, and she moved to Australia.

Charlotte "Lottie" Moon (1840–1912)

American Lottie Moon spent nearly 40 years as a missionary in China. Born in Virginia to staunch Baptist parents, she was educated at the Valley Union Seminary (later Hollins University), where she received one of the first M.A. degrees awarded to women at a Southern institution. She was a gifted linguist, speaking several languages including Latin, Greek, and Chinese. Her sisters were also highly educated, and one became a physician. Lottie chose a teaching career, working in schools in Kentucky and Georgia before deciding to open her own Cartersville Female High School in 1871. A year later, one of her sisters accepted a call to go to China as a missionary, and Lottie was influenced to join her. She traveled to China in 1873 to teach at a boys' school there. She taught at several schools before she left education in 1885 in order to evangelize full time.

Above:

Charlotte "Lottie" Moon, American missionary teacher in China.

Native American Schooling

Some boarding schools for Native American children had already been founded for the purpose of "assimilation" in the 18th century, and missionaries established many more during the 19th century. The schools promoted Euro-American habits and ideas and were supposed to "civilize" Native Americans. This impetus for educating Native Americans in Euro-American ways gained popularity. In 1819, the Civilization Fund Act provided funding to Christian societies and groups to establish schools for this purpose. In lightly populated areas in the West and on reservations, teachers also worked in small schools and in American Indian boarding schools. The Bureau of Indian Affairs also founded schools.

Below:

A group of native Americans at a Sunday School at Honor Mission, Michigan.

THE CARLISLE INDIAN INDUSTRIAL SCHOOL

In 1879, Colonel Richard Henry Pratt (1840–1924) established an Indian boarding school in Carlisle, Pennsylvania. Known as Carlisle Indian Industrial School, it was the first federally funded off-reservation boarding school for Native Americans and served as a model for many other such schools established in the country. Colonel Pratt believed in the fundamental equality of Native Americans with whites, and thought that forced assimilation was the best way to bring about their full and equal participation in American society. He believed education was the tool whereby such assimilation would be achieved.

Colonel Pratt's methods for cultural assimilation at Carlisle Indian Industrial School were later considered to be a form of cultural genocide, since the pupils from more than 140 tribes had to learn to speak English, take an English name, and dress in Euro-American school uniforms. Their hair was cut short, and they had to wear boots. Discipline was harsh, and the school was run like an army barracks. While some chiefs sent their sons to Carlisle to learn English and to be able to trade, many parents whose children were recruited for the school had no idea of the harsh regime to which their children were subjected.

To satisfy tribal leaders, groups of Native American chiefs were allowed to inspect the school at intervals. The first group of inspectors visited the school in 1880, and the event was photographed. Indeed, Carlisle Indian Industrial School was regularly photographed, as Pratt considered it to be a model school that could be imitated successfully. In addition to academic subjects such as mathematics, history, and geography, pupils also studied music. Also, sports was a major part of the Carlisle experience. There was a large gymnasium, and both the school football team and the school band were very successful.

Zitkala-Ša (1876–1938)

Teacher, writer, and political activist Zitkala-Ša's Sioux name translates as Red Bird, and she was also known by her missionary-given name Gertrude

Left:
A music teacher at Carlisle Indian Industrial School, Pennsylvania, Zitkala-Ša was an accomplished musician, and played at the Paris Exposition of 1900.

Simmons Bonnin. Her father was European-American, and her mother was a Native American from Dakota. Her father abandoned the family at an early stage, and Zitkala-Ša was raised on the Yankton Reservation in what would become South Dakota. When she was eight, a group of missionaries visited the reservation and recruited some children to take to a Quaker boarding school in Wabash, Indiana.

Zitkala-Ša received her high school diploma in 1895 and won a scholarship to Earlham College in Richmond, Indiana. In 1899, she took up a position as music teacher at Carlisle Indian Industrial School. An accomplished violinist, she played at the Paris Exposition of 1900 along with pupils from the Carlisle Indian Band. She also began collecting Native American stories and wrote extensively about the erasure of her native culture. She collaborated on an acclaimed opera, *The Sun Dance Opera* (1913), and her work was published in *Harper's Monthly* and *Atlantic Monthly*. Her book *American Indian Stories* (1921) provided insight into the effects of assimilation on Native Americans.

Aboriginal Education in Australia and New Zealand

Like Native Americans, the Aboriginal peoples in Australia and New Zealand had an oral tradition whereby culture, laws, history, and knowledge were passed within communities and kinship networks. "Teaching" was also accomplished by experience and observation. The impact of colonization included that indigenous culture and educational practices were forced to give way to the "civilizing" influence of European schooling.

AUSTRALIAN INSTITUTIONS

One of the first colonial education interventions in New South Wales, Australia, was a school called the Parramatta Native Institution, which was established by Governor Macquarie's government in 1814. Children were taught to read and write; girls learned to do needlework, and boys received instruction in mechanics and agriculture. In some instances, pupils had been removed from their families to be placed in the Institution. The first superintendent and principal instructor at the school was William Shelley (1774–1815) of the London Missionary Society. Upon his death, his wife, Elizabeth Bean Shelley, assumed the role of principal instructor.

From the 1830s, various Christian charitable groups and church missions established schools for Aboriginal children to teach basic literacy and to convert them to Christianity. For example, in 1838, the German Lutheran missionaries Christian Gottlieb Teichelmann and Clamor Wilhelm Schürmann established schools that taught lessons in the Aboriginal vernacular. However, this was an unusual innovation, and by the mid-19th century, teaching in schools for Aboriginal children was conducted through the English language with very few exceptions.

In 1848, a secular Board of National Education was established in New South Wales, and government-run schools operated alongside church and charity schools. However, Aboriginal people were denied access to state schools until the passing of the Public Instruction Act in 1880. There was a brief period in which Aboriginal children attended state schools until the establishment of the Aboriginal Protection Board in 1883. The Board had the power to move Aboriginal people into segregated government-run "reserves." Some Aboriginal children living outside

Below:

Aboriginal children in Mornington School, Queensland, Australia.

reserves were educated in nonsegregated schools, but their experience of schooling often included isolation and expulsion.

Christian Gottlieb Teichelmann (1807–1888) and Clamor Wilhelm Schürmann (1815–1893)

German missionaries Christian Gottlieb Teichelmann and Clamor Wilhelm Schürmann founded a Lutheran mission school for Aboriginal children in Adelaide, where teaching was conducted in the vernacular. Teichelmann was born in the German kingdom of Saxony, while Schürmann was from Hanover. Both were educated at Jaenicke's Missionsschule in Berlin, where they studied the classics, languages, and world geography in preparation for a life as missionaries.

The Lutheran Missionary Society of Dresden prepared them for their roles as founders of a school for Aboriginal children in South Australia. They were keen students of indigenous languages, and published *Outlines of a Grammar: Vocabulary and Phraseology of the Aboriginal Language of South Australia, Spoken by the Natives in and for Some Distance Around Adelaide* (1840). In 1840, Schürmann took up a government position as deputy-protector of Aborigines at Port Lincoln. He sought government support for an agricultural settlement and school for the Aboriginal population, and eventually succeeded in opening a school at Wallala in 1850, where instruction was given in the Parnkalla (Banggarla) language.

ABORIGINAL EDUCATION IN NEW ZEALAND

In New Zealand, the early 19th-century missionary schools taught pupils in the native Maori language. In 1847, an Education Ordinance was passed, requiring missionary schools to conduct classes in English in return for funding. However, armed conflicts between the state and the Maori over land rights known as the New Zealand wars (1845–72) led to the schools closing, and rather than help churches rebuild schools, the government passed the Native Schools Act of 1867 setting up secular state schools in Maori communities, which required that classes were taught in English only.

Above:

Girls and teacher at Yarrabah school, Queeensland, Australia. Illustration from Pitt's Children of Wild Australia, *1914.*

Universal Education

In the early 19th century, elementary education was mainly provided by charitable societies, by various religious groups, and by individuals running speculative ventures. This changed in many parts of the world, as support increased for the idea of free, nonsectarian public schooling, or "universal education."

NORTH AMERICA

In the United States, Horace Mann (1796–1859) was the "father of the common school movement" and a vigorous supporter of free universal education. Mann was largely self-taught, as he came from a poor family and rarely attended school. He eventually studied at Brown University, graduating as valedictorian in 1819. He later taught at Brown, but then pursued a legal and political career. In 1837, Mann was appointed secretary of the newly created board of education in Massachusetts. He threw himself into his work, visiting all of the schools in the state and examining their condition. Convinced of the need for a well-structured system of common schools, he founded and edited the *Common School Journal* in 1838, and articulated the principles that he believed should underpin mass education. He argued that schooling should

be available to all, and that the poor should not be excluded from education; teachers should be well trained and properly paid, and the curriculum should not be narrow in focus.

In 1843, Mann went to Europe to visit schools. He was especially impressed by the "Prussian system," which he later promoted in Massachusetts. The system was also adopted in schools in New York. The Prussian system promoted free primary schooling, professional training for teachers, funding for school buildings, and secular instruction that included developing a sense of national identity in pupils. As a system, it was admired for its efficiency, allowing large numbers of children to be taught literacy at a relatively modest cost, and Mann could see its value for the United States.

In 1852, Mann was appointed president of Antioch College in Ohio. He taught philosophy, economics, and theology there and continued to give public lectures promoting public schools. A popular teacher and college president, Mann employed the first woman academic to be paid a salary equal to that of her male colleagues.

THE BRITISH ISLES

The idea for a nondenominational state-supported system of mass education had been mooted in Ireland in the past, but it was Chief Secretary Lord Stanley who succeeded in getting the system off the ground in 1831 via a document that became known as the "Stanley Letter." The ideas contained in this letter addressed to the Duke of Leinster had consequences for not only Ireland, but also England and

the colonies. The letter provided the blueprint for a national system of schooling with a national board to manage the provision of funding toward school buildings. The national board also controlled the curriculum by devising graded reading books that teachers were obliged to use in all national schools. These books, which were well-made and produced in large quantities, found their way to schools in North America, where they were popular with teachers.

The schools were free, and their main aim was to promote the spread of literacy in the English language. In 1878, to support the achievement of this aim, a scheme known as "payment by results" was introduced. Under this plan, teachers were paid a basic salary supplemented via payments calculated on the basis of the examination performance of their pupils. The system encouraged teachers to use rote learning in the classroom in order to prepare pupils efficiently for the annual examinations.

The success of Ireland's "experiment" in national schooling influenced changes in education in England. The passing of the Elementary Education Act in 1870 established state-supported "board schools" in England.

In Scotland, teachers traditionally held a position of status in the locality, and their views on education reform and practice were reflected in policy. The *dominie* (schoolmaster) was an important figure, and a "lad of parts" (clever boy) from a humble village could aspire to becoming a teacher if he attended public schooling and worked diligently at his studies. This was a sentimental national ideal, but a popular one.

In Wales, a distinctively Welsh system that consisted of "circulating schools" had been developed by Griffith Jones (1684–1761) as early as the 1730s to spread literacy to the masses. Schools were held for three months in one location before moving on

Above:

Cookery class at a Horace Mann school in Tulsa, Oklahoma. The image was taken by the celebrated American photographer Lewis Hine.

to another location. The popularity of these schools greatly contributed to Welsh literacy levels by the 19th century. However, formal elementary education was not widespread in Wales until the second half of the 19th century.

EUROPE

In 18th-century Europe, the Kingdom of Prussia was one of the first countries in the world to introduce free, compulsory elementary or primary schooling. The *Volschule* was an eight-year course that offered basic reading, writing, and math skills, along with education in obedience and duty. From 1810, teachers were required to hold state certificates in education, raising teaching standards, and the state established teacher-training colleges.

A system of secondary schooling was developed during the 19th century with four different kinds of schools, academic or technical, and these were compulsory and free.

In the 1830s, the Prussian elementary system was introduced into France. In the 1880s, French Minister of Public Instruction Jules Ferry created *l'école républicaine*. This system required all children under the age of 15—boys and girls—to attend free-of-charge, secular schools designed to break the hold of the Catholic church on education. In the latter half of the 19th century, other European countries attempted to make primary education compulsory; however, children were often not sent to school, and the illiteracy rate was high.

Below:
Girls taking part in their school board elections, under the supervision of a teacher. From The Graphic, *1876.*

International Theories of Teaching and Learning

The 19th century saw the publication of many of the key texts on education theory that teachers today still study. Education was viewed as a science, the story of which required a rigorous approach. The development of the child's imagination, intellect, and physical competence greatly interested education theorists, and the discipline of pedagogy grew in stature. At the same time, the "art" of teaching was also of interest to educators, and the development of a "natural" and engaging teaching style was respected.

Above:

Swiss educator Johann Pestalozzi with pupils in a school in Stans, Switzerland.

Johann Pestalozzi (1746–1827)

Many of the principles that underpin elementary teaching today have been derived from the ideas of the Swiss educationalist Johann Heinrich Pestalozzi. He was influenced by Jean-Jacques Rousseau (see page 25), and emphasized the need for learning that included engagement with nature, physical activity, and work that is relevant and interesting to the pupil. The essence of the teaching method he developed is the gradual unfolding of the talents and abilities of each child. His curriculum included singing, drawing, model-making, and field trips. All these learning activities have both developmental and pedagogical value, and should be selected by the teacher to suit the abilities of the pupils.

Pestalozzi believed that teacher training should be approached in a systematic and scientific way. He produced a substantial body of writing, and his main education principles are explained in *How Gertrude Teaches Her Children* (1801). This book appeared while Pestalozzi was directing a school in Burgdorf, Hanover, Germany, where he remained until 1804. He then ran a boarding school at Yverdon-les-Bains, Switzerland, from 1805 until 1825. In these schools, he worked out his ideas, providing pupils with the three branches of education: intellectual, moral, and physical. Many international educators visited the boarding school in Switzerland, including Friedrich Froebel.

FREDERICK FROEBEL

Copyright, 1897, by C. W. Bardeen, Publisher, Syracuse, N. Y.

Friedrich Froebel (1782–1852)

Influenced by both Jean-Jacques Rousseau (see page 25) and Johann Pestalozzi (see page 70), the German educator Friedrich Froebel's teaching career included training elementary teachers and developing his own theories of infant education. In 1837, Froebel founded an infant school in Blankenburg, Prussia, which he named the *Kindergarten* (garden of childhood). His legacy to education was enormous, and the widespread popularity of

kindergarten schooling today reflects the success of his ideas. He emphasized the role of play in education and believed that learning could take place through play activities and singing. The kindergarten teacher should encourage children to express themselves rather than using drilling or rote learning.

To use play in a stimulating way, Froebel developed objects and toys that he called "gifts." Many adults today will recall having used these gifts in

their kindergarten schools. They include wooden spheres, boxes of cubes, cylinders, sticks, and rings. Each gift is numbered. Gift five, for example, is a box of cubes and prisms that can form a three-inch cube or be used to create other shapes.

John Dewey (1859–1952)

The American educator and philosopher John Dewey was born in Vermont. With a bachelor's degree from the University of Vermont and a doctorate from Johns Hopkins University, he became a university teacher at the University of Michigan. His studies in both philosophy and child psychology led him to develop his theories of progressive pedagogy. He believed schools and civil society had major roles to play in the creation of democracy.

He argued that the training of teachers should not merely be instructing them in a repertoire of teaching techniques and disciplinary strategies. Rather, teachers should learn how to share their passion for knowledge and how to foster genuine intellectual curiosity. Teachers, he believed, have a role in shaping civic society by teaching their pupils how to act wisely and effectively and by developing their intelligence. Skilled teachers are those who are aware of their pupils and adapt their methods. They learn to cope with the stresses and demands of the profession and remain passionate about their subject, so their students are always engaged and curious.

Above:

The kindergarten room at Des Peres School, St. Louis, Missouri, which was established by Susan Blow in 1876 as the first kindergarten in the United States. Note the Froebel banner on the wall and the "gifts" on the table.

> *"To the 'natural born' teacher, learning is incomplete unless it is shared."*
>
> John Dewey

Teaching and Change

Changes in the education and training of the teacher were a feature of the 19th-century education landscape. As pedagogy became a respected academic discipline, colleges and universities developed programs for teachers, and opened education departments. The schoolroom was increasingly seen as a place where social inequalities could be overcome, and education could play a real role in promoting democracy.

TEACHER TRAINING AROUND THE GLOBE

Teaching developed its professional status as training colleges and university departments took on the role of educating pre-service teachers. Before that, school teachers generally learned the skills of classroom management and some general principles of pedagogy simply by watching other teachers and imitating them.

In Ireland, formal teacher training was available as early as 1811 with the establishment of the Kildare Place Society (see page 48) and its training college. Another early teacher-training college, Mico College, was established in Jamaica in 1834.

In countries that adopted the monitorial system (see page 46), such as Britain and Ireland, an "apprenticeship" system existed in the first half of the 19th century whereby older pupils learned to teach by helping in the classroom.

Australian schools also used this system, and there pupils as young as 13 could apply to become a pupil-teacher. While teacher-training colleges grew in number in both Britain and Ireland in the second half of the 19th century, Australian training colleges only developed in the 20th century in Western Australia, Queensland, and Tasmania.

Japanese teacher training began with the establishment of "normal schools" (schools for teacher education) in 1872. Somewhat similarly, in the United States, training for teachers was offered in normal schools. Pennsylvania was the first state to require

Below:
Students at Teachers College, Columbia University, New York.

teachers to pass tests in reading, writing, and arithmetic before being appointed to a post. Locally administered tests were introduced into most states by 1867, and these tests included the "three Rs" and American history and geography. Throughout the 19th century, different states adopted different practices concerning teacher training, and the teaching profession did not become regularized until the start of the 20th century with the development of university departments of pedagogy.

American teachers also developed their professional skills by working at prestigious private "academies," the oldest of which is Andover Academy founded in 1778. Some of these schools were theological seminaries, such as Hampden Academy (1803). They usually educated the elite, and they followed classical curricula. At Delaware Academy (1819), for example, students studied Latin, Greek, Astronomy, and Mathematics. Delaware opened a department of common-school teachers in 1840. By the mid-19th century, many schools in the United States were recognizing the importance of training their teachers. With the spread of different pedagogic theories, education became a science and found its place within the universities. The first graduate program in education was established in 1887 at New York University and in the following year Teachers College, Columbia University, was founded.

Above:

Andover Academy, United States, founded in 1778, was a prestigious private school where American teachers honed their skills.

SEGREGATION AND INTEGRATION

In the United States, most early 19th-century education provision was racially segregated. Although some missionaries, such as the Ursuline nuns in New Orleans, promoted schooling for black children, most African-Americans received little or no education, and some states prohibited teaching enslaved African-Americans to read and write.

During Reconstruction, laws were passed in Southern state legislatures to establish public education. With the exception of desegregated public schools in New Orleans, the newly established schools were segregated by race. Black schoolteachers were trained, and colleges were set up for black students, including the Tuskegee Institute in Alabama, whose first leader was Booker T. Washington.

The impact of widening access to education for African-Americans meant they began to secure places in universities. People such as the educator and physicist Edward Alexander Bouchet were able to progress to a university and attain distinction in their fields.

Left:

A math class at Tuskegee Institute, photographed by American photojournalist Frances Benjamin Johnson in 1899.

Below:

A mathematical geography class studying Earth's rotation around the sun at Hampton Institute, Virginia. Photographed by American photojournalist Frances Benjamin Johnson in 1899.

Above:

Booker T. Washington, promoter of industrial education for blacks.

Booker T. Washington (1856–1915)

Born a slave in Virginia, Booker T. Washington and his family moved to West Virginia after emancipation. He worked in coal mines to earn money, and made his way to Hampton Normal and Agricultural Institute (now Hampton University), a school for freedmen. He also attended Wayland Seminary (now Virginia Union University). In 1881, he was appointed first leader of Tuskegee Institute, the normal school (teachers' college) in Alabama.

Washington was a prominent figure in black politics, popular with leaders in education, philanthropy, and business. He worked to raise funds to establish hundreds of schools and institutions of higher education in the South, and had the support of many self-made white philanthropists. He promoted industrial education for Blacks, believing that this could bring them both stability and wealth. To demonstrate the contributions of African-Americans to American society, he helped organize the "Negro Exhibition" at the 1900 *Exposition Universelle* in Paris, France, displaying photographs of students at his own alma mater, Hampton Institute.

Edward Alexander Bouchet (1852–1918)

The first African-American to attain a Ph.D. from an American university, Edward Alexander Bouchet completed his dissertation at Yale University in 1876. He taught chemistry and physics at the Philadelphia Institute for Colored Youth (now Cheyney University of Pennsylvania) for 26 years. He also taught at Lincoln High School, Ohio, and at Bishop College in Marshall, Texas. Both Yale and the American Physical Society have named awards in his honor.

Fanny Jackson Coppin (1837–1913)

Another African-American who taught at the Institute for Colored Youth was Fanny Jackson. Born a slave, she was bought into freedom by an aunt and managed to get an education while also working as a domestic servant. She entered Oberlin College in 1860 and graduated in 1865. Jackson became the first African-American woman to become a school principal when she was appointed to lead the Institute for Colored Youth in 1869. Her teaching

subjects were mathematics, Greek, and Latin, and in her 37 years at the Institute, she brought about many improvements in education and achieved her goal to promote industrial education alongside academic education.

Jackson was also the first African-American superintendent of a school district in the United States. She married a Methodist Episcopal minister, the Rev. Levi Coppin, and went with him to South Africa, where he ministered and she did educational work, including founding the Bethel Institute in Cape Town. They returned to the United States after a decade of missionary work, and she died in 1913. The Fanny Jackson Coppin Normal School, Baltimore was named for her in 1926.

Below:

Fanny Jackson Coppin, the first African-American female school principal.

Above:

The Girton Pioneers were the first class at Girton College, Cambridge, England, 1869.

financial independence, intellectual stimulation, and even travel.

When Emily Davies founded Girton College at Cambridge, England, it is unlikely she predicted that so many graduates would pursue a teaching career. Half of the 102 women who were educated at Girton between 1879–90 became schoolteachers, and 16 became college teachers. The very first class at Girton in 1869 became known as the Girton Pioneers. Several of them became teachers—Louise Lumsden became classics mistress at Cheltenham Ladies College, and later was the first warden of University Hall for Women at the University of St. Andrews (1895–1900); Jane Francis Dove became first headmistress of Wycombe Abbey School (1896–1910), and Louisa Maynard cofounded Westfield College and became its first head in 1882.

Other Girtonians went to America to do postgraduate research. There, some of the pioneering women's colleges were also producing many graduates who became teachers. Mount Holyoke (1837), Vassar (1865), Wellesley (1875), Smith (1875), the Harvard Annex/Radcliffe (1882), and Bryn Mawr (1884) provided America with many teachers.

Some of these American women viewed teaching as a way out of the routines of rural life. Alice Freeman Palmer, president of Wellesley College in 1882, strongly encouraged Wellesley students to think of entering the teaching profession. Within two years of her presidency, 71 percent of the senior class went into teaching. Freeman Palmer established satellite secondary schools to raise the standard of girls' education, and many of the Wellesley alumnae staffed these schools and hundreds of other schools nationally. Freeman Palmer became a noted expert on secondary education.

TEACHING AS A PROFESSION FOR WOMEN

The revolution in female education in the 19th century had a direct impact on the teaching profession—many of the first women to graduate from universities became schoolteachers. The option of a teaching career gave women the opportunity for

WOMEN TEACHERS AND PERSONAL ADVANCEMENT

Why was teaching so attractive to women? First, it was a profession open to them at a time when the other learned professions remained firmly closed. Second, it was considered a suitable job for a lady, as it required some of the caring virtues of motherhood. Third, teaching was a respectable form of employment, and it was a way for the daughters of lower middle class parents to move upward in social rank.

Not all women teachers attended college. For example, the distinguished educator Margaret Haley, who would eventually found the first American teacher's union, was the daughter of lower middle class Irish immigrants who were unsuccessful in business. Haley had to withdraw from private Catholic schooling for which her father had paid $85 per year in an attempt to prove his rising social standing. Margaret went straight into teaching at the age of 16 and sat for the county examination for elementary teaching certification. Her certificate ensured she got employment in the expanding public school system in Chicago.

Teaching was also attractive to women because it gave them the opportunity to work outside the home, to make strong friendships, and—occasionally—to travel to new places. For example, the American frontier offered many women the opportunity to forge new lives for themselves as teachers.

Mary Ann Graves was one such frontier teacher. Born in Indiana in 1826, she and her family joined a wagon train in 1845 and made their way to California. She married in 1847 and settled in the San Jose area. However, she turned to teaching to earn her living after her husband was murdered. She was the first schoolteacher appointed in Tulare County, and she went on to educate generations of children. Thousands of American women were frontier teachers, and they worked tirelessly for the children in their charge.

Right:
*Wellesley College President
Alice Freeman Palmer
(1855–1902).*

Above:

Art class at Queen's College, London.

HIGHER EDUCATION FOR WOMEN

Women were debarred from attending universities in most of the world until the mid-19th century. While some medieval women were scholars, and they clearly had benefited from university teaching, the formal opening of university education and degrees to women was a late 19th-century phenomenon. Perhaps unsurprisingly, once women attained university education, they were attracted to the teaching profession, securing posts as schoolteachers, headmistresses, and—to a lesser degree—university academics.

In 19th-century Britain, women attended lectures made available through cultural societies, scientific bodies, and at the Mechanics' Institutes and Work-

ing Men's Colleges. This was a form of adult education and did not prepare them to become teachers. These lectures became so popular with women that by 1839, women formed nearly a third of the audience at York and Sheffield. The lectures for ladies were a source of income for these institutes. For example, the London Working Men's College charged women five shillings per term for four classes per week, providing them with subjects such as bookkeeping, history, and geography.

The kind of lectures that attracted middle class girls and women were particularly popular with those who hoped to become teachers or governesses. However, these lectures were not teacher training, per se. Women began to recognize there

"The teachers of a school may aim merely to impart information; the teachers of a college must lead their pupils to the apprehension of principles ..."

F. Denison Maurice

Principal of Queen's College, London, England, 1848

Below:
Dorothea Beale, principal of Cheltenham Ladies College, and tireless supporter of professional training for women teachers.

was a need for separate women's colleges, and so two important institutions were founded in London: Queen's College (1848) and Bedford College (1849). Both colleges provided women with the kind of education that would help them secure work as teachers.

The decision to call Queen's a "college" and not a "school" reflected its aim to provide a higher level of education than was available more generally to women. Women who attended Queen's College testified to how exhilarated they were by the academic demands and the spirit of inquiry that surrounded them.

Among the first pupils at Queen's College were two women who would go on to play a leading role in promoting academic education for girls—Dorothea Beale and Frances Buss.

Dorothea Beale (1831–1906)

The daughter of a London surgeon and his wife, Dorothea Beale had the kind of education common to women of her class—she was taught at home until she was old enough to attend a fashionable boarding school. In 1848, she and one of her sisters were among the first women to attend the newly opened Queen's College, London.

Beale was a natural student, and she excelled at mathematics. She became a math tutor at Queen's College in 1849 and then became head teacher in a school attached to the college. In 1858, Beale competed with 49 applicants to secure the post of principal of the prestigious Cheltenham Ladies College (1854) in Cheltenham, Gloucestershire.

Above:

An illustration of the Stanley library at Girton College, Cambridge, England, the first residential college of higher education for women.

Dorothea Beale was a tireless supporter of the idea of professional training for women teachers, and she believed this was the only way to raise the standard of girls' education. She founded St. Hilda's College in Oxford as a residential teacher-training college for women. Beale also established a training department for kindergarten teachers.

Passionate about teaching, Beale was president of the Headmistresses' Association from 1895–97, and she was a vocal influencer in its cause—she gave evidence before a royal commission on education in which she staunchly supported academic education for girls and women.

Emily Davies (1830–1921)

When Emily Davies founded Girton College in Cambridge, England, in 1869, as the first residential college of higher education for women, further progress was made in providing academic teaching for women, and in widening the teaching opportunities for women. Davies was a strong supporter of her friend Elizabeth Garrett who wanted to study medicine. Garrett eventually succeeded in becoming the first Englishwoman to become a physician and surgeon in Britain.

Although academic women were frequently ridiculed in popular publications such as *Punch* magazine, Davies continued her commitment to education, becoming a member of the London School Board and publishing the book *The Higher Education of Women* (1866). With the support of women such as Frances Buss, Dorothea Beale, and the painter Barbara Bodichon, Davies established Girton College as a women's college with the aim of providing women with an education "equal to that of men." She was awarded an honorary doctorate by Glasgow University in 1901.

Left:

Emily Davies, educator and mistress of Girton College, Cambridge.

Above:

A 19th-century Punch *magazine cartoon portrays the new phenomenon of women graduates in their robes drinking tea while their male counterparts drink beer.*

From Slate to Tablet

For over two centuries teachers used slates in their classrooms to teach writing and arithmetic. In the first half of the 19th century, slates were replaced with paper. By the 21st century, the electronic tablet had arrived in schools.

The slate and stylus were students' tools from earliest times and were still in use in 19th-century classrooms. Slices of quarried slate were set within a wooden frame, and sometimes had a sponge attached by a string to wipe off chalk. In many 19th-century schools slates were shared, and pupils often spat on them and rubbed them with their sleeves to clean them, which contributed to the spread of infectious diseases.

Slate was also used to make the blackboards, or chalkboards, used by the teacher. These either stood on an easel or were mounted to the schoolroom wall. A disadvantage of the blackboard was the dust generated by chalk. When the whiteboard appeared in the 1950s, it was a cleaner option. At first, enameled steel was used, but this proved costly. Laminated board, painted vinyl, and acrylic coatings provided cheaper surface options by the second half of the 20th century. Dry-wipe markers are used, and a damp sponge or duster is used to clean the surface.

Today, the interactive whiteboard is commonplace. It is connected to a computer, and a projector displays the computer's desktop onto the whiteboard. Teachers and students use a stylus, mouse, or their fingers to control the device.

Before the electronic tablet brought back the stylus in a new form, the pencil replaced the stylus. Although graphite was discovered in England in the 16th century, mass-produced pencils originated in Germany. Nuremberg cabinetmaker Kaspar Faber produced wooden pencils in his spare time. This would eventually grow into the Faber-Castel company, founded in 1761. In the United States, Joseph Dixon opened a pencil factory in Jersey City in 1847, where he developed a machine that produced wood for 137 pencils per minute. His business succeeded; by the end of the 19th century, almost a quarter of a million pencils were used each day. However, another cabinetmaker is credited with having produced the earliest American pencils—William Monroe in Massachusetts in 1812.

First in use in the mid-18th century, copybooks became common in the 19th. Elementary teachers favored headline copies, where cursive fonts and writing samples were displayed on each page and the pupils copied them as neatly as possible.

From left to right:
Pupil with a slate; Roman mosaic showing a woman with a wax tablet and stylus; A.W. Faber pencils from the German company's 1897 catalog; a child using an electronic tablet.

Above:

A 21st-century teacher in Lyon, France, using an interactive whiteboard and electronic stylus.

Below:

Pages from a 19th-century headline copybook, with simple maxims for the pupils to copy. These popular copybooks also included a series used to teach drawing.

Right:

Contractors removing old chalkboards at Emerson High School in Oklahoma City discovered another set of chalkboards underneath, untouched since 1917.

VERE FOSTER'S COPY-BOOKS

VERE FOSTER'S Copy-books are issued in three styles of writing. (1) BOLD WRITING, a legible, cursive business hand, embodying the principles essential to fluent writing; (2) MEDIUM WRITING, in which the body

and the junctions effected so as to render such a method of writing natural and easy. The most important points to be observed by the teacher are:—

1. **Formation of the letter a.**—Commencing on the

The better part of valour is discretion.

Line from Bold Writing Copy-Book, No. 17.

The better part of valour is discretion.

Medium Series.

The better part of valour is discretion.

Same line as above, written in Style of Upright Series.

strokes are lighter and the slope rather less than in the BOLD SERIES; (3) UPRIGHT WRITING, in which the slope is less than in either of the other series, while still sufficient to keep the writing from settling into backhand.

The essential principles of Vere Foster's system may be briefly stated as follows:—

From the beginning of their training pupils are taught to write words **continuously**, that is, from end to end without lifting the pen, and the characters are formed

base-line with the *hair-stroke*,[1] the hand is carried up, then well to the right to form the top of the oval, then *back* a certain distance over the hair-stroke, round to complete the oval, and down for the down-stroke, and finishing the final hair-stroke at the upper line, as here shown in BOLD, MEDIUM, and UPRIGHT styles. All this is done *in one operation* with-

BOLD	*a*
MEDIUM	*a*
UPRIGHT	*a*

[1] The term *hair-stroke* is used for the sake of convenience, though Mr. Foster did not approve of very fine up-strokes, or *hair-strokes* as usually understood.

(Continued on page 3 of Cover.)

VERE FOSTER'S COPY BOOKS—BOLD WRITING SERIES. No. 6.

BLACKIE AND SON, LIMITED.

Abhor that which is evil.

A light heart lives long.

1 2 3 4 5 6 7 8 9 0   1 2 3 4 5 6 7 8 9 0

3 THE TWENTIETH CENTURY

Through two World Wars and economic depression, teachers shouldered responsibilities that far exceeded their classroom duties. The education profession was influenced by developments in psychology, and great strides were taken in the "scientific" study of teaching. Against a backdrop of social and technological change, teacher education embraced new theories and methodologies. The materiality of schooling changed too: at the century's start, children wrote on slates, but by the end, they would use computers.

The Changing Schoolroom

The schoolroom changed considerably across the 19th and 20th centuries. Equipment, seating, and the architecture of schools were modified and modernized. Changes reflected innovations in the wider world, and they also responded to new pedagogies and ideas about childhood. Students developed a greater sense of ownership of their schools, and the forbidding 19th-century classroom was replaced by a room where children displayed their work, stored their things, and put up seasonal decorations.

CLASSROOM FURNITURE

The school desk was redesigned many times from the late 19th and throughout the 20th century. Manufacturers were keen to capture the growing market for school furniture once compulsory education meant that greater numbers of children went to school. Desks were given names, such as the Fashion Desk (1880), and advertisements described the unique attractions of each design. Early versions had chairs and desks mounted together on steel frames. It was common to have an inkwell and a groove in which the pen would sit. Most schools favored two-seater desks as they were more economical on space and cheaper to buy.

Later developments included the single desk with a concealed box space underneath to store books. From the mid-20th century, some schools favored these single box-desks while others invested in movable and stackable tables and chairs along with school lockers for storage of both sports equipment and books.

SCHOOL DESIGN

The one-room school was an example of vernacular architecture, and it imitated features of the buildings that surrounded it. Early 19th-century schoolhouses in Ireland, for example, are very much like cottages or small houses. Later, when the National Board in Ireland supported the building of state-supported National Schools, standard models were designed, and then duplicated with minor variations. In the United States, the one-room schoolhouses that dotted the prairies were like small barns or wooden farmhouses. Schools that were built by wealthy donors, or by religious orders, were often large and impressive structures. Convents, for example, had to house not only the schoolchildren but also large religious communities, and boarding schools required substantial buildings.

In Britain in the 1870s, when universal education was introduced, thousands of new schools had to be built. Standardized designs were used, with the result that features such as red brickwork, gables, white paintwork, and high windows can be seen in hundreds of Victorian schools.

Mary Medd (1907–2005)

One of the foremost modernist architects was Mary Medd. Born in Bradford, England, she was educated at Bedales, one of the U.K.'s most exclusive public schools, and later in Switzerland, and began her architectural training at the Architectural Association in London in 1927. In 1941, she was hired by Hertfordshire's education officer to design huts in which school meals would be served. After World War II, she specialized in school architecture for Hertfordshire, and was unique among architects in making a point of consulting with teachers to find out what they wanted from school buildings. She went on to design many schools, always with a deep awareness for the needs of the teacher and pupils, and a great knowledge of the importance of school space in child-centered education. Her international reputation for school design meant her opinion was often sought for school design projects.

In the 21st century, it is recognized that school design needs to facilitate peer-to-peer learning, and

it should accommodate a range of learning styles. Good design can aid the teacher in the provision of more personalized educational experiences. This is helped by the incorporation of modular furniture and adaptable spaces, or "learning zones." The goal is to build sustainable "green" schools, where light, water, and nontoxic building materials are used resourcefully. This can be done while preserving older school buildings.

Above:

Burntwood School in London—by architectural practice AHMM—won the 2015 Stirling architecture prize. Note the airy double-height room, the informal table groupings, and the use of art and bold color.

"*Schools can and should be more than just practical, functional buildings— they need to elevate the aspirations of children, teachers, and the wider community. Good school design makes a difference to the way students value themselves and their education.*"

Paul Monaghan

Director, Allford Hall Monaghan Morris (AHMM)

The Study of Education

The 20th century saw the growth of education as an academic discipline. Many other theorists contributed to the lively debates that characterized the world of education, and the first university departments of education were established. Research in areas such as child psychology, curriculum studies, and subject pedagogies all contributed to the professionalization of teaching.

Below:

Austrian philosopher and founder of the Steiner-Waldorf schools, Rudolf Steiner in the 1920s.

EDUCATION THEORISTS

The late 19th century and the 20th century gave us many education ideas that have shaped schooling today. For example, the ideas of Rudolf Steiner can be seen in the Steiner-Waldorf schools, while the home-school movement has drawn on the ideas of Charlotte Mason. Jean Piaget developed his theories of cognitive development, and Jerome Bruner articulated his ideas on curriculum development. Some of the well-known educationists that have been studied by student teachers and graduate researchers include John Dewey (see page 73) Maria Montessori (see pages 94–96), Martin Buber (see page 97), Ivan Illich (see pages 98–99), and Paulo Freire (see page 98).

Buber acknowledged the natural creativity of the child, but also argued that children have a basic instinctual orientation to create or "originate"; they want to be involved in creating and ordering experience. This spontaneous creativity needs to come in contact with the teacher. The teacher influences, instructs, and criticizes, but the involvement of the teacher should be unobtrusive and dialogic. Dialogue between the teacher and pupil must involve real listening, empathy, and a willingness by both the pupil and teacher to learn from the encounter.

Rudolf Steiner (1861–1925)

Philosopher and writer Steiner founded his first school in 1919. Set up to educate the children of workers at the Waldorf-Astoria cigarette factory, the establishment put into practice Steiner's theories on developing the whole child. Teaching was through an artistic and practical approach that included classes in rhythmic movement, creative play, and wholesome food.

Today, there are Steiner-Waldorf schools and teacher training centers worldwide. In the United States, the schools are known as Waldorf schools, while in the U.K., they are more commonly known as Steiner schools. The school buildings are decorated with students' work, and the Steiner-Waldorf method encourages creativity and self-expression. The schools also emphasize respect for the world and for the self. Steiner urged teachers to stay with the same class grouping for middle school (ages 7–14), after which time the pupils would be taught by teachers with subject specialties.

Jean Piaget (1896–1980)

Swiss developmental psychologist Piaget's theories of cognitive development became widely influential in the 1960s, and popularized a learner-centered approach to teaching. Research on child development included studies of personality, self-concepts, linguistic development, and cognitive development. Piaget contributed much to developmental psychology, including his articulation of four developmental stages. He showed that children enriched their learning by reflecting on their own previous knowledge and organizing their learning in structures that become increasingly complex. Teachers, Piaget argued, should allow children to learn by discovery, rather than providing all of the answers and solutions.

Jerome Bruner (1915–)

American psychologist Bruner's work on cognitive learning theory has had significant influence. In the 1960s, he wrote several important works on how the curriculum could be improved, in particular how to redesign it so it didn't just focus on merely memorizing facts. Bruner said, "Intellectual activity anywhere is the same, whether at the frontier of knowledge or in a third-grade classroom.'"

He helped found the Head Start early childcare program and collaborated with the innovative preschools of Reggio Emila in Italy to improve educational systems internationally.

"Only education is capable of saving our societies from possible collapse, whether violent or gradual."

Jean Piaget, 1934

Above:
Swiss psychologist Jean Piaget, 1974.

Above:

Italian educational theorist
Maria Montessori.

Maria Montessori (1870–1952)

The educator whose name has become almost synonymous with early childhood education is the Italian medical doctor and teacher Maria Montessori. Her philosophy of education, known by her name, is used in schools all over the world. The Montessori Method was derived after careful study, which included the completion of a degree in medicine at the University of Rome. Montessori's medical training included the study of pediatrics and psychology, and these disciplines influenced her later work in education.

Upon graduating from university, Montessori worked with children who had disabilities, and in 1900, she became director of the *Scuola Magistrale Ortofrenica*, an institute that trained teachers to work with pupils with special needs. Montessori developed materials to use with the pupils and demonstrated that the children were—contrary to common belief—not only educable, but also often capable of academic success.

She continued to develop her ideas in an approach she termed "scientific pedagogy," and in 1906, she took over the role of director of the *Casa dei Bambini* (Children's House) in Rome, where she applied her methods to children who did not have special educational needs. Montessori's classrooms were designed with small-size tables and chairs for the children, and special cabinets of equipment to use in learning activities. Bookshelves were low enough for children to access, and equipment was child-size. Children learned how to take care of themselves and their environments by doing practical tasks such as learning how to tie their shoelaces and how to use a sweeping brush. Handwashing, care of pets, and keeping things clean and orderly were also part of the education of the Montessori pupil. These activities, she believed, would help children to become independent and self-reliant.

Montessori also experimented with how children could learn to read and write. She used letters cut from sandpaper and picture cards with labels—ideas that teachers routinely use today in early childhood education.

"*The greatest sign of success for a teacher is to be able to say, 'The children are now working as if I did not exist.'*"

Maria Montessori

Above:
Maria Montessori visiting a school in London, England, in 1946.

"Preventing war is the work of politicians, establishing peace is the work of educationists."

Maria Montessori

Above:

Eight-year-old girls working on a pin map of the continent of Africa at Henson Valley Montessori School, in Maryland, 2006.

Within two decades of the opening of the first *Casa dei Bambini*, Montessori education was established in schools in countries including Switzerland, the U.K., France, China, Australia, Japan, Korea, and the United States. In 1909 her ideas were published in a book entitled simply *The Montessori Method*. It became a best-selling work in the United States, and has been translated into many languages.

While Montessori's teaching methodologies have occasionally been criticized for being rigid, and some of the classroom activities have been described as lacking in spontaneity, the principles of her methods are still used in schools around the world and Montessori training is a specialized area of teacher education recognized by the Association Montessori Internationale.

Martin Buber (1878–1965)

Born in Vienna, Martin Buber was a student at the University of Leipzig where he advocated the political advancement of Jews. He was appointed to the Chair of Jewish Philosophy of Religion at the University of Frankfurt in 1923. With the rise of Nazism, he was forced out of this position, but he continued to promote Jewish education in Nazi Germany until he was prohibited from lecturing in public. He emigrated to Palestine in 1938, and became a professor of anthropology and sociology at the Hebrew University in Jerusalem.

For Buber, education was connected with freedom and with the free expression of ideas. The role of the teacher was to facilitate learning and exploration, rather than to impose views. Teachers should be spontaneous and authentic. Buber was less concerned with the specifics of pedagogy and more concerned with how teachers gave their pupils a sense of identity, and enabled them to act with responsibility and love.

"I take him who listens to me by the hand and lead him to the window. I open the window and point to what is outside. I have no teaching … I carry on a conversation."

Martin Buber

Left:

Austrian philosopher Martin Buber, 1963.

"What the educator does in teaching is to make it possible for the students to become themselves."

Paulo Freire

Above:

Brazilian educator Paulo
Freire, 1979.

Opposite:

Social reformer Ivan Illich,
1985.

Paulo Freire (1921–1997)

Brazilian educator Paulo Freire criticized schooling for the way in which it operated by "banking" information in pupils, rather than teaching them how to be critical and questioning. Freire was a schoolteacher for several years before becoming an academic and writer. His career included becoming a visiting professor at Harvard University in 1969, and this was followed by a period as special education advisor to the World Council of Churches in Geneva. He returned to Brazil in 1980 to become Secretary of Education for São Paulo.

Freire's best-known work is *The Pedagogy of the Oppressed* (1970), in which he argued that the education of oppressed peoples should allow them to regain their dignity and become liberated. Importantly, the oppressed should have a role in determining this education. Education was a political act, he argued, and teachers should be conscious of the politics of education and of the ideas that they bring into the classroom.

Ivan Illich (1926–2002)

Born in Vienna, Austria, Ivan Illich was a leading educational thinker in the 1960s, a period in which the role of the school in creating a capitalist society was criticized by radical thinkers. He has been described as "one of the most outstanding figures of our time." The father of "deschooled" education, Illich condemned out of hand both the school system and the schools. Educated at the University of Florence in Italy and later at the Gregorian University in Rome, Illich became a Catholic priest, working first in New York and later as vice rector of the Catholic University of Puerto Rico in Ponce. Following a disagreement with the bishop of the diocese, he returned to New York in 1960 to take up a professorship at Fordham University. Continued controversies and disagreements with the church resulted in Illich leaving the priesthood in 1969.

His educational writings were critical of institutionalized education, and he believed that schooling and education were, essentially, opposed concepts. Schools, he argued, reproduced values that

sustained a society where those with cultural capital continued to derive the greatest benefits. Schools supported a myth that what they offered had intrinsic value, while teachers delivered a curriculum that was a "product," and students were caught up in a race for diplomas, degrees, and qualifications. Real learning, he believed, included the means to educate and empower the self. Museums, libraries, theaters, and the free exchange of skills and ideas between peers were all valuable sources of education for Illich. His ideas have, to some degree, found expression in ways that people support their own learning today via social and educational networking and the use of information freely available through the Internet.

"Teaching, it is true, may contribute to certain kinds of learning under certain circumstances. But most people acquire most of their knowledge outside school ..."

Ivan Illich

Teaching Conditions

While educational philosophers articulated a need for stimulating experiential education and theorists recognized the important role of the teacher in creating a good education experience for pupils, the reality at the start of the 20th century was that many teachers around the world worked in difficult conditions. Better schools and new methods of teacher training were needed.

In the United States, high school principal Edward Goodwin gave a realistic appraisal of how teachers experienced schooling:

"The teacher should have time for abundant physical exercise in the open air, and for such recreation as affords him needful rest and pleasure. This is not only his right but his duty. Children are as soft as clay in the hands of a teacher who possesses an abundance of vitality and good nature. But how many teachers in the village high schools of New England can even approximate such a condition? As a class, they are seriously overwrought. They spend their days in the most harassing kind of labor in the schoolroom and their nights in tutoring some ambitious pupil, or in preparing for the six, seven, eight, or more recitations that must be conducted the next day. The debilitating effects of such a life are easily discernable. No one should wonder that such teachers are nervous, irritable, and despondent. If young men are to be induced to enter the small high schools and remain in them, this stress and strain of overwork that depresses the spirits and impairs the health of conscientious and faithful teachers should be removed."

Edward J. Goodwin of Newton, Massachusetts, May 1895.

Right:

A mixed-age (5–13) class at a colored school in Anthoston, Kentucky, at the turn of the century. Although 27 children were registered for the school, only 12 enrolled; the teacher expected 19 once work was over. "Tobacco keeps them out, and they are short of hands," he is reported to have said.

There were tens of thousands of one-room and two-room schools dotted across the United States, Canada, and Australia. They were also common in Europe, and the teacher often had responsibility for more than just teaching. They invariably had to light the fire on winter mornings, take care of repairs, and keep the school tidy.

Past pupils who had attended small schools in the West Texas counties in the 1930s and 1940s recalled the chores that had to be done by pupils and teachers to keep the school open. "The teachers always had to build the fire every day," Bessie Cleveland recalled about her school in Pleasant Valley. "The teacher would have to see that the boys had brought in enough coal and kindling for the

next day." Juanita Vinson recalled her school, called Oak Grove, north of Caddo, Texas, which was run by a husband-and-wife team. "The wife taught the younger children, and her husband served as principal as well as teaching the older students … [and] the people in the community also used the school building to make mattresses in." Leo Clegg's memories of schooling at that time included the many pranks the boys played on their teachers. The boys would take .22-caliber ammunition shells, wrap them up in paper, and put them into the stove that heated the schoolroom. "Then whoever done it would be readin' a book, actin' like nothin' was goin' on, and d'rectly there would be an explosion. The shell would go off … one feller put a whole box full in the stove once."

Above:

Boys and girls take a class in English or penmanship, at the Carlisle Indian School, Carlisle, PA, 1901.

Opposite:
Sloyd pedagogy promoted wood- and metalworking skills.

Sloyd Education

The sloyd educational system of handicraft education became popular in nineteenth-century Finland and also in Sweden, where it became a compulsory subject in 1955. By then, it had also become popular in Norway and Denmark. The word "sloyd" derives from the Swedish word *Slöjd*, and refers mainly to doing work by hand in the areas of woodwork and textiles.

Right:
Otto Salomon (1849–1907) was an early proponent of sloyd in Sweden, where it is still part of the curriculum.

OTTO SALOMON

THE SLOYD APPROACH

The kind of manual training promoted by educational sloyd aims at improving children's dexterity and technical skills. Through making useful objects by hand, children acquire skills that can be used in their general education. Sloyd, therefore, teaches children to be industrious and contributes to character-building.

Students begin with paper craft, which includes cutting, gluing, and folding, and paper sloyd is not unlike the Japanese art of origami. When the teacher considers the student ready to move to more difficult work, new skills are developed. Controversially, young children are taught how to use knives and chisels during woodworking sloyd. The teacher's knowledge of each student is crucial, as the teacher needs to decide the appropriate tasks for the child. The purpose of including sloyd in the curriculum was to allow students to develop skills by completing tasks that became incrementally difficult. Today, sloyd is part of the curriculum in schools in Sweden, Norway, Denmark, and Finland.

Otto Salomon (1849–1907)

Born in Gothenburg, Sweden, Otto Salomon was the best-known early proponent of educational sloyd, and articulated the pedagogical approach to be used by teachers. He was a student at the Institute of Technology, Stockholm, before being appointed director of the Sloyd Teachers Seminary in Naas, Sweden. There, he popularized the sloyd movement, which he wrote about in his book *The Sloyd in the Service of the School* (1888). In *The Teacher's Handbook of Sloyd* (1892), he explained methods for teaching the different exercises and provided advice on the student's posture and the correct materials to use in class. The book became the main teacher-training text for instructors.

SLOYD AROUND THE GLOBE

The influence of sloyd pedagogy had reached other countries, including France, Scotland, and Ireland, by the end of the 19th century. Many Icelanders attended the Sloyd Teachers' Seminary in Naas, Sweden, and they brought the pedagogical craft to

Iceland, where it became popular and continues to be a school subject. Swedish sloyd was also known to Russian educators such as Karl Ziroul, who visited the Naas school and returned to teach sloyd at St. Petersburg State Higher Teacher Seminary. By the end of the 19th century, it was being taught in 10 of the 12 Russian education districts. Italy also sent groups of teachers to Sweden to study sloyd, and dozens of Italian publications on sloyd appeared by the early 20th century. Sloyd also spread to the United States, and there was a Sloyd Teacher Training School in Boston attached to the North Bennet Street Industrial School (now known as the North Bennet Street School).

SLOYD IN CONTEMPORARY FINLAND

In 2010, the Finnish National Board of Education assessed learning outcomes in sloyd, along with other elements of ninth-grade education. A questionnaire completed by 257 sloyd teachers indicated that, generally, in lessons teachers use learner-oriented working methods rather than teacher-centered instruction. Traditional sloyd together with the field of technology education are elements of the Finnish education system that develop both the personal and psychomotor skills of the school students.

Below:

Although the use of the knife in woodwork classes was not universally popular, the pedagogy suggested that pupils should learn how to work safely with tools.

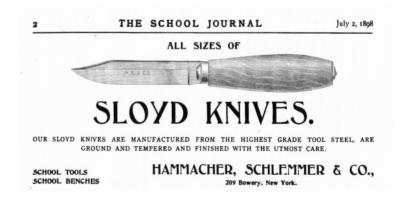

The Impact of Social Research on Teaching

In the early 20th century, social researchers and psychologists were interested in teaching methods. Some hoped to improve education provision for pupils with learning difficulties, while others' aim was to motivate pupils to stay in school and improve their life chances.

Below:

The American psychologist G. Stanley Hall

G. Stanley Hall (1846–1924) and Theodate Smith (1860–1914)

American pyschologists such as G. Stanley Hall and Theodate L. Smith recognized that children were often demotivated because they could not concentrate in class. Hall and Smith wrestled with ideas about children's attention span, concluding in 1907 that it was a complex issue that needed a child-centered solution.

Elizabeth E. Farrell (1870–1932)

Special education pioneer Elizabeth E. Farrell was born in New York to an Irish immigrant family and was educated by the Sisters of Charity. Their influence on Farrell was such that she became determined to help people in need. She trained as a teacher at the Oswego Normal and Training School,

"Voluntary attention is a complex development involving an effort of will … the best educational methods demand a study of children's interests, and an adaptation of the school routine to them."

G. Stanley Hall and Theodate Smith

and then went on to do further studies at New York University, and at Teachers College, Columbia University. She began teaching in New York at Public School No. 1, an "ungraded" school where pupils of different ages and abilities were in class together. In 1906, she was made Inspector of Ungraded Classes and director of special education.

It was at Teachers College that Farrell developed the nation's first special education curriculum in 1915. She began to test schoolchildren to determine the cause of poor education achievement, and she shared her research with other professionals, including students at Teachers College. She became first president of the International Council for Exceptional Children in 1922. Farrell died 10 years later, at the age of 62. In New York, Public School No. 116 has been named the Elizabeth Farrell School in her honor.

Helen M. Todd

While Helen M. Todd was not an educationist, she conducted informal research in 1909 to find out why youths in Chicago preferred to work in poorly paid factory jobs rather than attend school. Todd was a factory inspector, and she surveyed 500 child laborers who had dropped out of school. Among the many responses that she received were comments such as, "You never understands what they tell you in school, and you can learn right off to do things in a factory," and "The boss he never hits you; or slaps your face, or pulls your ears, or makes you stay in at recess." Todd's informal survey suggested that poor urban children found school to be an unhappy and even humiliating experience. Such work, along with that of social scientists, helped teachers and policy makers to better understand how children experienced school and how teachers needed skills and training to work with diverse student groups.

Todd's research also illustrated the fact that teenagers formed part of a poorly paid labor force when they should be in school. For example, it is known that almost 10 years later, some 7,000 boys in Michigan harvested a beet crop worth $5 million. The need for compulsory education legislation was clear: by 1920, it would be in place in every state.

"It is the boast of Americans that every child has the opportunity of school education, but it is true that many children—through no fault of their own—get nothing from education. Not education, but the right education should be our boast."

Elizabeth Farrell

Mari-Luci Jaramillo (1928–)

An early proponent of bilingual/bicultural education, Mari-Luci Jaramillo is known internationally for her research and work to promote the education of Latinos. She was born in New Mexico to low-income parents who urged their children to "study, study, study." Jaramillo excelled at school, and—having married and had three children—she eventually completed a degree at New Mexico Highlands University. She taught at a remote mountain school, later completing a master's degree at night. From her teaching experience, she saw many Latino children suffered from the lack of bilingual/ bicultural education provision, and she embarked on further research. Her Ph.D. research identified a need for radical curricular reform to diminish disparities in educational achievement.

Jaramillo traveled widely in the 1960s, speaking out on the needs and contributions of Latinos, and participating in the civil rights movement. In 1977, President Carter appointed her U.S. ambassador to Honduras. In 1980, she moved to Washington, D.C. as deputy assistant secretary for inter-American affairs, and she continued to travel widely to speak on social issues. She has received many awards for her work, including the PRIMERA award from the Mexican-American Women's National Association, for being the first Latino woman to be appointed as a U.S. ambassador.

Innovators and Teaching

Some early 20th-century educational innovations would have a lasting impact not only on schools, but also on educational thought. During the course of the century, educators experimented with different ways of developing schools that would respond to the needs of children and society.

Patrick Pearse (1879–1916)

Irish nationalist and teacher Patrick Pearse was educated by the Christian Brothers in Dublin and at University College Dublin (UCD). Although he became a lawyer, he had a great love of teaching and of the Irish language. He taught Irish at Alexandra College in Dublin, lectured in Irish at UCD, and was an active member of the Gaelic League, which promoted the language. His education philosophy was expressed in his writings, including *The Murder Machine*, and in the schools he founded.

Pearse was harshly critical of the kind of education available to Irish children, which had been impoverished by British interference and the erasure of the Irish language, culture, and history from the classroom. He wrote a damning criticism of Irish education under British rule in *The Murder Machine*:

"There is no education system in Ireland. The English have established the simulacrum of an education system, but its object is the precise contrary of the object of an education system. Education should foster; this education is meant to repress. Education should inspire; this education is meant to tame. Education should harden; this education is meant to enervate. The English are too wise a people to attempt to educate the Irish in any worthy sense."

Pearse founded a bilingual school for boys called St. Enda's at Cullenswood House in the Dublin suburb of Ranelagh to promote teaching through the Irish language. He took the pupils on field trips to parts of Ireland where Irish was still spoken, and fostered a love of Irish literature and culture in his charges. He was also involved in founding a school for girls, St. Ita's.

Pearse wrote poetry and prose and was a well-known political pamphleteer. He was spokesperson for the 1916 Easter Rising, and it was he who read the Proclamation of the Irish Republic outside the General Post Office on Easter Monday that year. Immediately following the Rising, Pearse was court-martialed and executed by firing squad.

Rabindranath Tagore (1861–1941)

Education ideas in 20th-century India were influenced by the man who became Asia's first Nobel Laureate, Rabindranath Tagore. Tagore believed the curriculum should emerge organically to reflect one's surroundings. The intellectual and the aesthetic elements of development were equally important. Students should study history, not to see which wars had been won, but to understand how to break down religious and social barriers. He founded a small school at Santiniketan, West Bengal, in 1901, which later became the Visva-Bharati University, and he dedicated the rest of his life to the project. There, he tried to create an alternative model of education that developed human values alongside intellectual development. Teachers and students were involved in social work and in promoting cooperatives.

Left:

*The Indian writer
Rabindranath Tagore
founded a school in West
Bengal in 1901 to promote
his education model that
focused on social as well as
intellectual development.*

A.S. Neill (1883–1973)

Alexander Sutherland Neill was a Scottish teacher and education philosopher whose ideas were given expression in the school he founded called Summerhill. Neill's experience of schooling in Edinburgh had included being taught by his parents. His father, like many *Scots dominie* (the term for a Scottish schoolmaster) at that time, was a strict disciplinarian. This may have influenced Neill in his later determination that Summerhill should be a happy place where children did not fear their teachers. Neill was a poor student. However, his father took him on as an apprentice schoolmaster, or pupil-teacher, and he eventually went to teacher-training college and then to the University of Edinburgh, where he studied English literature. With the outbreak of World War I, Neill served as an army officer. He returned to education after the war and taught at a progressive school in Dresden, Germany. In 1924, he returned to England to found Summerhill boarding school together with his wife, Margaret, who was his lifelong supporter.

Underlying Neill's education philosophy was his belief that "being happy is what matters most." At the school he founded, authoritarianism was avoided, and self-governance was promoted. Students made decisions that affected the whole school community at a weekly community meeting. To respect their autonomy, Neill did not force them to attend lessons; rather, they attended if they wished to do so. The school was not without its critics, both externally and from within the student body. Some past pupils said they rarely chose to go to class; some did not learn to read properly, and others later said they were unable to apply to universities because of their poor academic education. Other past pupils have praised Summerhill for allowing them to enjoy school while learning the true meaning of democracy.

Neill was author of 20 books, including *Summerhill: A Radical Approach to Child Rearing* (1960). The school continues today under the leadership of Neill's daughter, Zoë Neill Readhead.

Right:

Headteacher Zoë Neill Readhead at Summerhill School, England, 1999. Readhead is the daughter of the school's founder, A.S. Neill.

"If the emotions are free, the intellect will look after itself."

A.S. Neill

Above:
Educational philosopher A.S. Neill at Summerhill, the school he founded to put his progressive views into practice.

Education and Change

The latter decades of the 20th century saw rapid change in education and in the professional lives of teachers. The impetus to find the "best modern way" was felt by educators, and everything from school design to teaching methods was reviewed.

DEVELOPMENT IN THE UNITED STATES

While the drive toward increasing pupils' test scores might have been behind the work of teachers in the United States in the 1960s and 1970s, the pupils they taught had cultural reference points that often seemed startlingly new. Beatlemania, rock

music, and the popularity of television affected the way youths engaged with their world. Modern techniques introduced in the 1960s included harnessing the television to support classroom instruction. Teachers also used slide and movie projectors, record players, and cassette recorders to teach languages, literature, and music.

Influenced by theorists such as John Dewey (see page 73) and Maria Montessori (see page 94), schools were increasingly built with open spaces, large windows, and moveable furniture. The kind of experiential learning promoted by Montessori and Dewey required a more flexible approach to classroom planning. Though many schools still arranged the desks in rows, the *New York Times Magazine* ran a feature in 1971 that described how much classrooms had changed in the 20th century. Elementary school teachers now move between small groups of children, sitting at their level to work on vocabulary cards, and they arrange the tables differently to do activities. Secondary school teachers involve the students in laboratory work, field trips, and classroom activities rather than dictating facts from the front of the room.

There was a greater interest in making learning active rather than passive, and an increased understanding of the importance of self-directed learning on the part of the students. Teachers continued to do the kind of planning and management tasks they have always done, usually without counting the time it takes.

"I'm starting to make plans for the end of the year. I want to clean out all desk drawers; to sort out all old ditto masters and worksheets in the file cabinet; to get rid of all the

"The three R's of our school system must be supported by the three T's—teachers who are superior, techniques of instruction that are modern, and thinking about education, which places it first in all our plans and hopes."

President Lyndon B. Johnson, 1965.

Above:

An open-plan classroom at Eveline Lowe Primary School, London, England. In modern schools from the 1960s, pupils sit in groups at tables rather than at individual desks in rows.

unused forms; to sort out ten years of boxes ... I spent some time writing a final newsletter for the parents. I tried to outline most of the things we've done this year and I made suggestions for summer activities ... I took an old sandbox over to the Teachers' Center, where I'll try to repair it this summer. I need to tear out all the rusted metal, build a new bottom and lining, and seal it with polyurethane."
Extract from Lynne Strieb, *A (Philadelphia) Teacher's Journal* (1985)

Maycie K. Southall (1895–1992)

The teaching career of Maycie Katherine Southall spanned more than 50 years, including two world wars. It was, therefore, a career that saw considerable change, including the move from rigid schoolrooms with rote learning to child-centered classrooms in which teaching was underpinned by the growing field of education research.

Born in Tennessee, Southall was raised in relative comfort on a farm. From an early age, she was interested in reading and books and, like many other children at the turn of the century, she attended a small one-teacher school. She went on to become a teacher in a one-room school in Coffee County, Georgia, in 1911. Her enthusiasm for her work was exceptional, and she organized not only her schoolroom but also the wider community attached to the school. She held fundraising events, sold eggs to buy books, and conducted classes both indoors and outside, encouraging the pupils to plant flowers and growing vegetables in the schoolyard.

Southall recognized in herself a need to do further study, and she enrolled at George Peabody College for Teachers in Nashville in 1918. Upon graduating from Peabody in 1920, she held a position as state supervisor of education in Raleigh, North Carolina. It proved a challenging time as she traveled around the state giving demonstrations at schools on a wide variety of topics, including new areas such as standardized testing and child-centered education. She also continued her own studies, completing her doctorate at George Peabody College for Teachers in 1929. One of a tiny number of women with this qualification, she was appointed to the academic staff at Peabody as professor of educa-

tion. Her career at the college spanned 35 years, during which she became a leading figure in the academic study of elementary education. She ran summer conferences on childhood education, and her research and teaching attracted students from China, Korea, Brazil, Japan, and Germany. While she was demanding of her students, she was also immensely generous and encouraging.

Southall was elected to the Educational Policies Commission of the National Education Association in 1943 and went to the White House for three major conferences on children and youth. Among her particular strengths as an educator were her knowledge of the teacher-education process, including school supervision, and her ability to promote interdisciplinary and intercultural education.

Above:

Leading U.S. educator Maycie Southall at a juvenile deliquency hearing in 1955.

Above:

The teacher leading this class of fourth-grade children at the Donatus Elementary School in Bonn, Germany, in 2012 will have had a minimum of three years of university education.

THE TEACHING PROFESSION AROUND THE GLOBE

Canada had experimented with model schools in the late 19th century, where novice teachers learned their profession by teaching pupils between the ages of 5 and 18. This training system died out in the early 20th century in most places, other than some remote provinces. "Normal" schools flourished, where teachers-in-training learned the principles and methods of teaching, which they would put into practice in the classroom. In the 20th century, teacher education became part of the university, with education departments providing the curriculum. Teachers typically specialize in elementary, middle, or secondary school programs, and others specialize in subjects such as music or physical education. Education in Canada has contributed to its prosperity and it has generally been well-resourced.

TEACHING IN GERMANY

Germany has also benefited from its education system, though its teacher-training system has sometimes been criticized for being conservative. New standards for teacher training were established in 1990. Three or four years of university education are required for those who want to teach in elementary and secondary general schools. Those who want to teach in secondary schools must study for five years. German secondary schools are known as *Hauptshule*, *Realshule*, and *Gymnasium*. *Hauptschule* offer all students a basic education, while students who want to attend the more academic *Realschule* or *Gymnasium* need to have good marks. After the age of 16 or 17, *Realshule* pupils either go on to an apprenticeship or to the *Gymnasium* schools, which offer education for university-bound students. The school curricula and textbooks must receive state

approval, and some teachers feel this diminishes their scope for innovation. The profession attracts considerably more women than men and, as in other countries, they have increasing responsibilities.

TEACHING AND CHANGE IN HONG KONG

Hong Kong is an example of a country where the teaching profession has changed rapidly in the second half of the 20th century. As Hubert O. Brown of the University of Hong Kong wrote in *Schooling in Hong Kong*: "Not so long ago … teachers had a secure, government-subsidized job with few professional demands or risk of unemployment, but they also had little personal challenge … To use an idiom from China, teaching was an 'iron rice bowl.'" But today the "rice bowl" has disappeared, and teachers have challenges and responsibilities in managing schooling and developing curricula. They also have opportunities for personal advancement.

Teaching has thus become an attractive career option for graduates, with the result that between 1986 and 1996, more than 18 percent of each graduating class from the University of Hong Kong became teachers. For some who came from nonprofessional families, becoming a teacher represents a step up the social ladder, and there is a high level of job satisfaction among teachers. The teaching profession is a relatively young profession, and the overwhelming majority of primary and secondary teachers have been professionally trained. A challenge in Hong Kong education is the tension between the traditional Chinese respect for conformity and authority and the contemporary need for creative and innovative approaches to learning and life.

Teachers carry a relatively heavy teaching load and also have additional duties such as leading co-curricular activities. Approximately 90 percent of all teachers, from kindergarten to university, are members of the Hong Kong Professional Teachers' Union, which offers workshops for teachers and runs a number of cooperative services.

Teacher Education and Training

Interest in the scientific study of education resulted in many universities opening schools of education and establishing chairs. Teacher training colleges also provided professional education for teachers.

TEACHER EDUCATION IN THE UNITED STATES

In Europe, the chair of education at University College Dublin was founded in 1909, while Harvard University established its Graduate School of Education in 1920. The New York School for the Training of Teachers, founded in New York in 1887 by the wealthy philanthropist Grace Hoadley Dodge (1856–1914) and educator Nicholas Murray Butler (1862–1947) for the training of teachers of the poor, laid the blueprint for the education of teachers and the scientific study of education in the United States when it became affiliated with Columbia University in 1898. Renamed Teachers College, students benefitted from the teaching of John Dewey (see page 73), the proponent of "experiential education." And it was at Teachers College that the field of educational psychology was developed under the influence of Edward Lee Thorndike (1874–1949). Thorndike, along with the Russian psychologist Ivan Pavlov (1849–1936), used animal models to develop his theories of behavior and human learning.

In 1929, George S. Counts, professor of education at Teachers College, sought to anticipate how the discipline of education would progress in the 20th century. His predictions would prove accurate: *"When in the year 2000 the historian writes his account of the period through which we are now passing, how, I often*

Left:
Edward Lee Thorndike, who was instrumental in developing the field of educational psychology at Teachers College, Columbia University, New York.

Right:
Russell Hall—a late 19th-century building—at Teachers College, Columbia University, New York, as viewed through the park gates across the street.

Above:

Queen Mary, consort of King George V of Great Britain, visiting the Froebel Institute, London, England, in February 1923.

Opposite:

A science class for trainee teachers at Digby Stuart College, Roehampton, England.

wonder, will he appraise the various educational tendencies of our generation. He will no doubt have something to say about the extraordinary extension of educational opportunity, the structural reorganization of the educational system, the almost universal concern with curriculum making, the differentiation of the program of higher education, the so-called progressive education movement, the development of teachers' colleges, the tremendous growth in educational expenditure, the widespread interest in the scientific study of education, and numerous changes in the structure and procedure of our schools and colleges. From his vantage point in time he will be able to assess in terms of their fruits that vast medley of currents and movements which now disturb the educational consciousness."

TEACHER TRAINING IN BRITAIN

In Britain, the 20th century saw teacher education becoming much more rigorous as the old pupil-teacher apprentice system was replaced by formal training. People who wanted to become teachers could either attend a teacher-training college or go to a university training department that provided training for university graduates.

Some teacher training colleges specialized in particular methods, while others had a distinctive ethos. For example, training in the methods of Froebel (see pages 72–73) was provided over a three-year term at the Froebel Educational Institute in London. And a prominent Catholic training college was founded by the Society of the Sacred Heart in Roehampton, London. It moved to North Kensington in the west of London in the early 20th century, and distinguished speakers at the college included Maria Montessori. The college returned to its first home, Roehampton, in 1946 and was named Digby Stuart College after two of the nuns who had been instrumental in its development.

By the 1970s, private training colleges found themselves under threat of closure, and Digby Stuart College merged with other colleges, including Froebel, to form the Roehampton Institute of Higher Education. In 2004, it became the University of Roehampton.

"Teachers believe they have a gift for giving; it drives them with the same irrepressible drive that drives others to create a work of art or a market or a building."

A. Bartlett Giamatti

Hard Times—War and Depression

Throughout World Wars I and II and the Great Depression, teachers not only worked in schools, but they also took on many additional responsibilities. On reduced pay, some fed and supported their pupils. Many were drafted or volunteered for service during the two world wars, while others left retirement to return to the classroom.

"The present war has brought a peculiar opportunity to American teachers ... and at the same time it has laid upon them a great responsibility ..."

U.S. National Board for Historical Service

Teachers and pupils played many roles in support of their own country's involvement in the war. In school kitchens, food was prepared and canned for shipment to feed men at the front, while teachers also coordinated sewing groups in which students made surgical dressings and clothing. School gardens were used to grow vegetables. In the United States School Garden Army, 1.5 million children raised crops and helped to promote the home-gardening movement.

Male teachers signed up to serve overseas, with the result that retired teachers were encouraged to return to work in their place. Districts that had refused to hire married women teachers before the war changed their policy and were happy to welcome them back into the workforce.

In Britain, schoolteachers were considered to have a particularly important role in instructing children in useful skills during the war years and in teaching them to be fit and healthy.

"The present war has brought a peculiar opportunity to American teachers of European history, and at the same time it has laid upon them a great responsibility. Their subject is more vital to Americans than ever before. By proper selection and emphasis of topics, they can instruct their pupils so that they will have a better understanding of present-day conditions and therefore of the reason why the United States is taking part in the war. Through the pupils they will reach many parents, and if the teaching is sound, they may be an effective factor in the country's political development."
U.S. National Board for Historical Service, 1917.

Above:

French pupils continue learning in a bomb-damaged building, in Barcy, Seine-Maritime, France.

As part of the British Empire, Canada was automatically at war from August 1914. Before the war, 1.4 million Canadian schoolchildren studied literary and historical materials that glorified the British Empire, though this was not a perspective that was approved of or accepted by everyone. However, with the outbreak of World War I, teachers generally endorsed the widespread view that civilians and soldiers should support the Allied war effort. In schools, teachers and students who enlisted were admired and respected.

War-related teaching materials were produced to support the position of the Allied cause. Students read *The Children's Story of the War* by Sir Edward Parrott of the British Parliament. They also learned about technical and tactical elements of battle, and kept scrapbooks filled with pictures of zeppelins, planes, soldiers, and tanks. Composition classes included written exercises on "Canada and the War," and the women's charitable organization the Imperial Order of Daughters of the Empire sponsored essay competitions on this theme.

However, as historian Kristine Alexander has noted, some teachers were concerned their students should not think patriotic teaching was a way of glorifying hatred.

In 1916, in a magazine for teachers called *The School*, Helena Booker, a teacher in Hamilton, Canada, wrote of the dangers of imprinting acts of hatred in the minds of children:

"We feel a great reluctance to bring so unhappy a subject before such young minds … So if we speak of war let it be with the sole purpose of teaching patriotism, a love of our own country, not a hatred of our enemies—a positive, not a negative, thing."

New Zealand would send 100,000 troops to Europe to support "King, Country and Empire." Meanwhile at home, teachers had to prepare students to be fit, healthy, and ready to do whatever might be expected of them. Boys were taught how to shoot and how to march. Girls and boys did physical drills, and all were involved in supporting the troops by fundraising, knitting warm scarves and socks, and writing letters to the soldiers.

In Britain, cadet activities, physical drills, fundraising, knitting clothing, and writing letters to soldiers were also part of the school regime.

In Germany, teachers and pupils were also expected to support their war effort. While in occupied Europe, teachers had to contend with the effects of displacement from bombings and nearby fighting on their pupils.

Below:

Children at Te Aroha Public School in New Zealand hem the edges of handkerchiefs for soldiers in June 1916.

Above:

First Lady Eleanor Roosevelt visits the childcare school at Vassar College and distributes glasses of milk to the children in New York in 1933.

THE GREAT DEPRESSION IN THE UNITED STATES

"It is pitch dark and forty below zero when we start the fire that modifies the temperature in our one-room school … At eight thirty we ring the bell and light the gas lamps. Most of the children have arrived and are in their places although school does not commence until nine. It is still ten below zero in the schoolroom when the flag is saluted and school opens … Rich voices rise in melody and a thick fog rises in the room; the frozen desktops become white with frost. As they sing, the children hold their inkbottles in their hands, alternately blowing on them and singing. We watch the bottles. When sufficient ink has thawed, we start the penmanship class."

Edward L. Keithahn, public school principal, Kale, Alaska, February 1932.

When the Wall Street stock market crashed in the fall of 1929, the country entered a period of deep economic depression. At first, schools seemed to be surviving the hard times, and school enrollments were up in 1930 and 1931. While only 25 percent of youths went to high school before the Great Depression, school attendance doubled during the 1930s as employment opportunities vanished. But schools struggled; education budgets were cut, schools were closed, and teachers were made redundant. In Chicago, for example, half of the elementary school principals lost their jobs in an attempt by the school board to cut salary expenses. Yet it was in Chicago that teachers rallied to feed thousands of pupils. On April 8, 1931, the *New York Times* recorded: "It appears that principals and teachers in many schools have for several months been contributing from their salaries in order to provide free lunches for hungry children … Meantime the [Chicago] Board of Education announces that it has exhausted its fund for the payment of teachers and other educational purposes."

Rural schools fared particularly badly during the Depression. They already had the poorest buildings and the highest truancy rates, and teachers were often paid very low salaries. Thousands of rural schools closed. Some states were badly affected such as Alabama where 85 percent of public schools had closed by 1933 with the consequent loss of teachers' jobs.

For those teachers who continued to find work during the Depression, conditions deteriorated. Sales of textbooks dropped drastically throughout the

United States, with the result that teachers had to work with books that became outdated and worn. Pupils often came to school hungry, and were incapable of working.

"Well this little boy fell out of his chair. Just fell out of his chair, just like this. I said, 'Get up off that floor and get back in your chair right now,' and he did. This child got back in his chair, and then he did it again. I hadn't said three words, and he collapsed again. So I walked to the door, and I motioned him to come outside. He got up and came out there, and I said, 'Rudy, what did you have for breakfast?' He said, 'I didn't have no breakfast.' I said, 'What did you have for supper?' He said, 'I had a little bit of beans, but they wasn't enough, and I didn't have many beans.' You cannot teach a hungry child."
Interview with Ina Dingus Cowan in *The Empty Schoolhouse: Memories of One-Room Texas Schools* by Luther Bryan Clegg.

When weather was severe, children and teachers often could not get to school at all. At other times, adults might show up from time to time to catch up on lessons that they had missed over the years. Pupils were withdrawn from school to help with farm work or with caring for small children. In an oral history interview with writer L.B. Clegg (*The Empty Schoolroom*), A.B. Lampkin recalled attending school in the 1930s:

"I went to school in Anson, in what was called then the Colored School — two rooms. One side was the high school and the other side was the elementary ... We were a little bit different because the black school didn't start up until about Christmastime because it stayed closed until cotton pulling was over. I don't know how we got anything accomplished."

When Franklin D. Roosevelt was elected president in 1933, his efforts to regulate the economy and create employment included targeting out-of-work youths and drawing on the labor of teachers. Teachers were hugely important to the success of the National Youth Administration (NYA) established in 1935 when Eleanor Roosevelt successfully lobbied her husband to create the NYA by executive order. The NYA gave financial aid to youths to stay in school in return for work. They provided training and skills to unemployed young people, supporting white, black, and American Indian men and women. Teachers who were members of the Work Projects Administration (WPA) taught school subjects as well as courses in metalwork, masonry, secretarial skills, home nursing, and childcare.

WPA teachers also taught adult education classes—in 1937 in New York City, some 70,000 adult learn-

Below:
A 1930s poster for free trade and technical day and evening classes sponsored by the Adult Education Project, W.P.A., and the Board of Education.

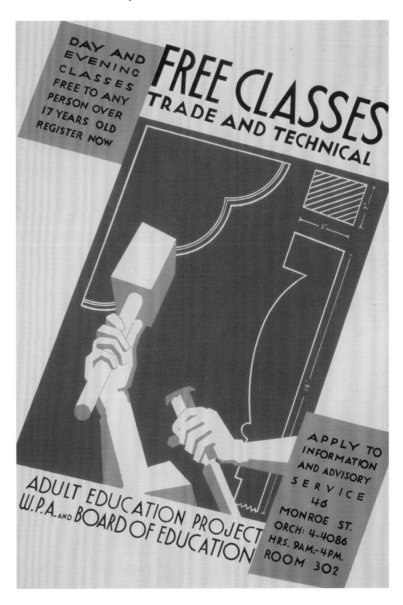

Above:

Physical fitness became important at a time when children were often undernourished. Drills are performed at a school in New Zealand in the 1930s.

ers were being educated by teachers employed by the WPA. They used settlement houses, churches, public schools, and private houses to teach classes in vocational and academic subjects. Across the period 1933–1938, the WPA teachers taught about 1 million adults to read.

Teachers were also very important in supporting families affected by the severe drought in the Southwest in 1934. Lack of rainfall, together with winds that blew dust storms, caused the prairie regions including those in Texas, Kansas, and Colorado to become known as the "Dust Bowl," also referred to as the "Dirty Thirties." Some 200,000 people migrated to California looking for work and a new life, where they would camp on roadsides in temporary homes. Teachers, using their own money, often fed migrant school children and tried to teach them, even though school attendance was erratic.

Teaching during the Depression in New Zealand

In New Zealand at the start of the 20th century, women comprised a majority of primary school teachers and about 40 percent of all secondary teachers. However, men held most of the senior positions in the teacher-training colleges, the schools, and in the Department of Education. They were also paid more than women—in 1929 women teachers had an average annual salary that was around 40 percent less than that earned by the male teachers. Women teachers were cheaper sources of labor, yet when the Depression hit New Zealand, they were the first to be laid off.

The use of a "marriage bar" had been adopted in the U.K. in the wake of economic crisis in 1921. It was now adopted in New Zealand as the education boards were given the authority to dispense with the services of married women teachers who did not depend on their income for a livelihood. The teacher-training colleges were temporarily closed as an economic measure. Once they reopened, women could return to teacher training, and they were in a position to provide relief teaching during World War II.

Dorothy Carkeek had trained at Wellington Training College and got a position as the sole teacher in a school in Longacre Valley in the 1920s. When she married, she left teaching. However, she later got work as a relief teacher. She described her upbringing as very harsh, saying "… we were as poor as crows." But she believed that this prepared her for working with poor children. "I thought being poor was good for a teacher. Wherever I go, I always get the scruffy kids to teach, and I don't mind because I can understand what it is to be hard up and not have things."

New Zealand teachers recalled living on very little during the Depression. They walked everywhere, and they brought food from their farm homes with them if they went teaching in another town. Traveling teachers boarded with local families, often sharing a bedroom, as this was the cheapest form of accommodation.

Education in Britain during the Great Depression

When the United States stock market crashed in 1929, Britain was struggling to pay for the effects of World War I. The impact of the Great Depression on Britain was severe as the value of exports plummeted, unemployment rose rapidly, and the pound was devalued. Communities in the industrial North of England and in Wales suffered particularly badly. In London and the Midlands people fared better as construction work and the growing automobile and aircraft industries provided work.

The minimum school leaving age was set at 14 in 1918, and children attended elementary or grammar schools. The wealthy upper classes sent their children to distinguished fee-charging public schools such as Eton and Harrow, while middle and upper-middle class families favored smaller fee-charging schools such as that featured in the 1930s novel *Goodbye, Mr. Chips* (see page 132). The relative stability enjoyed by children in such institutions was shattered with the outbreak of World War II.

Left:
At Britain's elite schools, pupils such as these boys from Harrow, were protected from the privations experienced by other children. However, many families who lost their fortunes after the Wall Street Crash had to withdraw their sons from private schools.

WORLD WAR II: TEACHERS FOR VICTORY

When war broke out in 1941, teachers and pupils all over the world found themselves, once again, trying to survive conflict. Those who were not involved in active service often worked to support the war effort.

American Teachers' Experience

In the United States, schools were harnessed in the preparation of young people to cope with an emergency. Schools furthest west were deemed more vulnerable to Japanese bombing, and pupils had to be ready to evacuate. In Hawaii, schools remained closed until February 1942, and upon reopening, they issued gas masks to children.

Teachers did far more than provide schooling during the war. They were involved in instructing children in issues such as rationing, and some taught Morse code for wireless radio and two-flag semaphore. Schools became involved in homefront efforts such as the sale of war bonds, making goods for servicemen, and gathering scrap metal.

High schools developed courses to meet wartime needs such as lessons on explosives, water purification, nutrition, map-reading, first aid, and navigation. When the age of eligibility for the draft was lowered from 21 to 18 in 1942, teachers tried to respond to the pressure to provide accelerated programs so students could graduate early. The school day was lengthened, and some schools added summer programs. All of the academic activity in schools took place against the additional need to support the war effort. For example, Chicago's public school teachers and students collected 1.5 million pounds of scrap metal for the war effort in 1942.

Some American teachers worked in the internment camps set up as part of the Japanese-American "relocation" that commenced in 1942. Many of the teachers were poorly paid Japanese-American graduates who were evacuees, and they helped to teach some 30,000 Japanese-American children who had been evacuated to barracks such as the Manzanar Relocation Center in eastern California. The War Relocation Authority reported in 1942 that no relocation center had been able to obtain the required quota of trained teachers. The schools were poorly equipped, and sometimes, teachers and pupils had no chairs or desks.

> *"We teachers must believe in the importance of our work. We must regard ourselves as full partners in the war effort and must do our work with an impelling sincerity and patriotic zeal."*
>
> Maud Frothingham Roby
>
> *Principal, Shepherd Elementary School, Washington, D.C., January 1943*

Left:

An aeronautics course for women held in Washington High School in Los Angeles, California, 1942.

TEACHING
is war-work, too

American Education Week
Nov. 5 to Nov. 11
VISIT YOUR SCHOOLS

THIS POSTER CONTRIBUTED BY WAMSUTTA MILLS, NEW BEDFORD, MASS.

Above:

An English school teacher demonstrates to her pupil how to fit his gas mask, 1940.

British Teachers' Experience

English schools were severely disrupted during the war, not only because of bombings, but because of the need to evacuate children from cities where heavy bombing could be expected, such as London and Manchester. The plan for the evacuation of children was known as Operation Pied Piper. Schools were central to the coordination of the evacuation process as schoolchildren assembled and were given their gas masks and an identifying label to wear around their necks. Teachers played a role in coordinating this part of the war effort, preparing guidelines for parents on what to pack for their children, and accompanying groups of children on the trains and buses that took them to places that were deemed low-risk for bombing raids. Some children were evacuated to other parts of the British Empire, such as Canada.

Many teachers went with the evacuated pupils to rural areas, and city schools were closed and handed over to the Civil Defence Forces. The shortage of city schools meant that children who had not evacuated often went without schooling. The problem was exacerbated as male teachers were conscripted into the armed forces. Schools in rural areas became overcrowded, and some used a "shift" system, whereby local children were taught in the morning shift and evacuees were taught in the afternoon shift. Teachers had to be flexible, economical, and very resourceful. Summer holidays were reduced. Michelle Magorian's novel *Goodnight Mister Tom* provides some insight into how children experienced school during the war.

Canadian Teachers' Experience

In Canada, the war directly affected education as thousands of students enlisted. In addition, schools were obliged to economize as supplies and equipment were cut, and teachers left for the war. Once again, teachers educated young people about the war, as they had done during World War I.

Teachers and students supported thrift campaigns to salvage metal and rubber, and they ran countless fundraising events. They sewed supplies for hospitals and made clothing for servicemen and for war orphans. Students in Montreal made 15,000 arm splints for the Red Cross, and worked on the building of scale models of aircraft used in the training of fighter pilots. In high schools, boys undertook cadet training. Teachers and students listened to the war reports of the Canadian Broadcasting Association, and worked together on projects to support the war effort.

As the historian Anne Millar has put the case: *"School activities in support of the war served two purposes. They helped demonstrate commitment to the war effort and they also provided an opportunity to teach children and youth about the values of thrift, hard work, perseverance, and the necessity of safeguarding democratic values and traditions. While lamenting the circumstances, educators recognized that the war provided an opportunity to instill in young Canadians a sense of responsibility for the future of their nation."*

TEACHING AFTER WORLD WAR II

The return home of servicemen led to an increased demand for college places and teachers. In the United States the G.I. Bill of Rights gave veterans access to loans and grants while they enrolled in higher education. The lives of women teachers changed dramatically. While they had been central to the war effort, they were once again considered secondary workers. The use of a marriage bar gave employers the right to dismiss married women. In Britain, the marriage bar in teaching was lifted in 1944, and in Ireland, it was lifted for primary school teachers in 1958. France did not introduce a marriage bar, while in parts of Australia, a marriage bar remained in force until the 1970s. In the United States, marriage bar policies were adopted by the majority of local school boards until the 1950s.

Above:
Preparing children for evacuation from London to the safety of the countryside, a teacher at the Myrdle School in Stepney, London, comforts a distressed pupil.

Teachers in Fiction

Many novels about teachers have been adapted for screen, stage, and television. It is easy to forget the origins of some of these dramatic re-creations. Novelists have examined the teaching life with its challenges and joys, setting their work in colleges, schoolrooms, and even in the playground.

THE TEACHING LIFE

In June 1934, a warm yet serious treatment of the teaching life was cautiously published in the United States by Little, Brown and Company. Publishers were reluctant to take risks on new work during the Great Depression, but *Goodbye, Mr. Chips* became an instant success, with many reprints (and a British edition went to press in fall of the same year). The huge sales of the book, in both the United States and the U.K., made author James Hilton famous. The story concerns a kind and quietly intellectual schoolmaster at a small British boarding school for boys. His is a conventional life, but he is greatly loved by many generations of schoolboys. James Hilton had attended the Leys School in Cambridge, England, and it is probable that the book was loosely based on life at that boarding school. *Goodbye, Mr. Chips* was made into a film twice, in 1939 and 1969.

Below:

British author James Hilton (1900–1954), seated, at a signing for his best-selling book Goodbye, Mr. Chips, *published in 1934.*

Left:
Muriel Spark, Scottish author of the 1961 novel The Prime of Miss Jean Brodie, *at work in 1960. Her book was made into a successful film (see p.147).*

TROUBLED SCHOOLROOMS

In his novel *The Blackboard Jungle* (1954), Evan Hunter examined the life of a teacher in a New York vocational high school. Hunter is also known for his screenplay of Hitchcock's *The Birds* (1963), and both works have nightmarish qualities. In *The Blackboard Jungle*, Richard Dadier is the teacher who finds himself caught up in the nightmare world of interracial gang culture. Although he is a Navy veteran, he still struggles to control his students and teach them, but eventually he wins their respect. The novel was made into a film with Glenn Ford in the leading role.

A decade after Hunter's depiction of a troubled classroom, Bel Kaufman situated an epistolary novel in another American inner-city school in *Up the Down Staircase* (1964). The central character is a teacher, Sylvia Barrett, who wants to share a love of English literature with her indifferent students. While she struggles to succeed in the school and almost abandons her job, she eventually realizes that she is having a positive effect on some students. Like *The Blackboard Jungle*, *Up the Down Staircase* was made into a successful movie.

TEACHER-PUPIL RELATIONSHIPS

The year 1961 saw the publication of another sensitive, and often witty, portrait of a teacher in Muriel Spark's *The Prime of Miss Jean Brodie*. Set in 1930s' Edinburgh, the novel looks at the relationship between a teacher, Miss Brodie, and her preferred students, known as the "Brodie girls." The six girls who she has chosen for her special attention experience a more liberal and intellectually rigorous education than other pupils. At first, they respect Miss Brodie, but eventually the reader learns that they betray her. Brodie is a memorable teacher, nonetheless, and the novel is a classic on the theme of teaching. In 2005, *Time* magazine listed the novel as one of the 100 best English-language novels published since 1923.

Jean Brodie is not always a likeable character, yet she elicits the sympathy of the reader. Barbara in *Notes on a Scandal* (2003) by Zoë Heller is similarly both unpleasant yet deserving of pity. The novel focuses on how the life of a younger teacher, Sheba, is destroyed when she has an affair with a 15-year-old pupil. Barbara manipulates Sheba once she discovers the illicit relationship and becomes consumed with jealousy.

Above:

Irish teacher turned novelist Roddy Doyle.

A TEACHER'S EXPERIENCES

The tribulations of a male teacher are explored with great sensitivity in *Stoner* (1965). The novel enjoyed a warm response when it was reprinted in 2003, attracting a new generation of fans for American writer John Williams. William Stoner's schooling, college years, and career as an English professor provide the scaffolding for a story about one man's dreams, desires, and disappointments. Stoner is raised on a poor farm in Missouri, but his parents manage to send him to a university to study agriculture. He is drawn toward poetry, and decides to switch to the English degree program. He eventually secures a post in the university as an English professor, and is a popular teacher who enjoys his work, even though he is often demoralized by department politics and the petty vanities of his colleagues. Stoner's deeply unhappy marriage and his affair with a younger academic add a compelling storyline to this beautifully written novel.

Teachers are also central to many other novels including *Plum Wine* (2007) by Angela Davis-Gardner, which looks at a young lecturer at Tokyo University, and *Ms. Hempel Chronicles* (2008) by Sarah Shun-lien Bynum, in which a newly beginning English teacher struggles to find out what is needed from her to succeed.

PRIZEWINNING TEACHER-AUTHORS

The Nobel Prize winning poet Seamus Heaney was not the only Irish writer to begin his adult life as a teacher. Several others who began their careers as teachers became hugely successful and internationally known authors, winning a range of awards for their work.

John McGahern won scholarships at school, and eventually went to St. Patrick's Training College, Dublin, to train as a primary school teacher. He taught for a while and began writing. His works included *The Dark* (1965), which was originally banned in Ireland and resulted in him losing his teaching post. He wrote many other novels, including *Amongst Women* (1990), which was nominated for the Man Booker Prize. In 2003, *That They May Face the Rising Sun* (2001) was nominated for the IMPAC Award. The same year, he won the Irish PEN Award. McGahern has also been awarded two French literary awards, the *Chevalier des Arts et des Lettres* and the *Prix Etranger Ecureuil*.

Irish-American author Frank McCourt's *Teacher Man* (2005) charts the story of one man's teaching life. It is autobiographical, drawing mainly on the author's teaching experiences in Stuyvesant High School in New York City, where the author taught English and creative writing. McCourt eventually published a very successful memoir *Angela's Ashes* (1996), which won the Pulitzer Prize for Biography or Autobiography (1997).

Another Irish teacher who became an award-winning writer is Roddy Doyle. Doyle's novel *The Commitments* (1987) first propelled him to fame when it was made into a successful film in 1991. His subsequent novels included *The Snapper* (1990), *The Van* (1991), and *Paddy Clarke Ha Ha Ha* (1993), which won the Man Booker Prize. Doyle has credited his teaching years at Greendale Community School, Dublin, with having provided some of the inspiration for his work.

William Golding (1911–1993)

Perhaps best-known for his novel *Lord of the Flies* (1954), Golding was first an English teacher. Golding studied English at the University of Oxford and then joined the Royal Navy to serve in World War II. He fought on a destroyer, and participated in the invasion of Normandy on D-Day, and his experience of war influenced his exploration of innocence and evil as depicted in *Lord of the Flies*.

After the war, Golding took a teaching appointment at Bishop Wordsworth's School in Wiltshire, where a plaque commemorates his time there as a schoolmaster between 1945–1962. His success as a writer, and the successful film adaptation of *Lord of the Flies* (1963), meant he could give up teaching to concentrate on his writing. In *Lord of the Flies*, a group of schoolboys become stranded on a deserted island. Without the guidance of their teachers and parents, they gradually lose self-control and become savage in their behavior toward each other.

Golding, like Heaney, is one of the most celebrated of all writers who were teachers. He won the Man Booker Prize in 1980 for *Rites of Passage*, and was awarded the Nobel Prize for Literature in 1983.

Below:

Briton William Golding, author of The Lord of the Flies *(1954), pictured in 1964.*

Above:

The 1981 TV serialization of Brideshead Revisited *was based on British author Evelyn Waugh's 1945 novel. The still shows Jeremy Irons as Charles Ryder standing in the quad of Hertford College, Oxford.*

CAMPUS NOVELS AND UNIVERSITY TEACHING

The college campus has provided dozens of novelists with a backdrop for their fiction, and academics have been portrayed variously as comic or romantic figures, artists, and even murderers. In some cases the campus appears fleetingly in the work, while other novels allow the university experience to form a backdrop to the unfolding story.

In Evelyn Waugh's *Brideshead Revisited* (1945), the central characters—Charles Ryder and Sebastian Flyte—meet at Oxford University. Charles is studying History at Hertford College when he meets Lord Sebastian Flyte and his extended group of eccentric and colorful friends.

Though the Oxford years form only a small part of the novel, they are made memorable by the exploits of Flyte, Ryder, and their friends, and they shape Ryder's future. While *Brideshead Revisited* was made into a feature film in 2008, it was the 11-episode television series produced by Granada Television in 1981 that attracted huge audiences and made a star out of the actor Jeremy Irons, who played Ryder. The Oxford scenes, shot on location at the university, displayed the beauty of the City of Spires, and showed the students punting on the river, cycling through the narrow cobbled streets, and partying with abandon.

Accounts of student days at Oxford and Cambridge are to be found in many novels, from Dorothy L.

Sayers's *Gaudy Night* (1935) to *Solar* (2010) by Ian McEwan. The two university cities have provided stunning backdrops for film adaptations of novels and biographical writings, including the *Inspector Morse* series from the novels by Colin Dexter and the movie *Shadowlands* (1993), in which Oxford academic and writer C.S. Lewis was played by Anthony Hopkins. A biographical account of the life of Cambridge Professor Stephen Hawking was recently released as a film titled *The Theory of Everything* (2014).

The American campus and faculty feature centrally in *The Groves of Academe* (1951) by Mary McCarthy. The novel, set in the fictitious Jocelyn College, is a satire on university life, portraying academics as vain and manipulative. McCarthy, who was briefly a lecturer, became a very successful author and critic, and won many awards including the National Medal for Literature in 1984. In the more recent *On Beauty* (2005), Zadie Smith also exposes the flaws of university academics, especially of the central character, Howard Belsey, who teaches at the fictitional Wellington College. *On Beauty* was shortlisted for the Man Booker Prize in 2005 and won the Orange Prize for Fiction in 2006.

COLLEGE TEACHERS AND COMIC NOVELS

There are several comedic novels set on campuses, including *Lucky Jim* (1954) by Kingsley Amis and Tom Sharpe's *Porterhouse Blue* (1974). Both novels take a shot at academia, portraying university dons as snobbish and occasionally foolish. In Sharpe's novel, the head porter at a fictional Cambridge college leads a rebellion against the changes brought about when a new master and his wife arrive at the college. Kingsley Amis set his novel in an anonymous British redbrick university, where a young history lecturer rebels against the pretensions of academic life.

Perhaps the best-known comic novels about university teachers are the campus triology by David Lodge. The novels appeared to acclaim between 1975 and 1988, and are titled *Changing Places: A Tale of Two Campuses* (1975), *Small World: An Academic Romance* (1984), and *Nice Work* (1988). Lodge was

a lecturer at the University of Birmingham, and also spent time as a visiting professor at the University of California, Berkeley. Lodge's professional experiences influenced his writing. The novels in his campus trilogy provide a hilarious account of the exploits of a modest British academic, Philip Swallow, and his exuberant American counterpart, Morris Zapp, whose aim is to be the best-paid humanities professor in the world.

Below:
British writer Zadie Smith, seen here promoting her campus novel On Beauty *(2005).*

Above:

Antonia White, British author of boarding school novel Frost in May *(1933).*

BOARDING SCHOOL TEACHERS AND ADULT FICTION

While boarding school fiction is well-known among British and American juvenile readership, there are also a number of highly regarded adult novels set in boarding schools.

Antonia White's *Frost in May* (1933) is set in a convent boarding school, the Convent of the Five Wounds, modeled on the exclusive Sacred Heart school that White had attended at Roehampton in England. White had been expelled from school for writing the start of a novel that was perceived as improper. This forms the basis of the story in *Frost in May*, when the central character, Nanda, has a similar fall from grace in the eyes of the nuns who teach her. Her teachers include Mother Radcliffe, Mistress of Discipline, who prepares the girls for life by teaching them to become "accustomed to hardship and ridicule and ingratitude."

The novel is written with a clarity and honesty that has caused critics to compare it to James Joyce's *Portrait of the Artist as a Young Man* (1916), which was also autobiographical and included reference to Joyce's education at the distinguished Jesuit boarding school Clongowes Wood College in Ireland. In both novels, the intellectual and religious awakening of the young pupil is influenced by their schooling.

In Kate O'Brien's *The Land of Spices* (1941), there are echoes of *Frost in May*, as it is also set in a Catholic boarding school for girls. O'Brien, like White, had attended a convent boarding school. She draws on her years at Laurel Hill Convent to create a context in which the central character, Anna, will learn about human frailty and adult sexuality. The Reverend Mother emerges as a wise and caring woman who shows great sympathy for children who are raised by parents who are indifferent to them.

American novels for adult readers have also included the boarding school as a locus of activity, and its teachers as central to adolescent growth. In *A Separate Peace* (1959), John Knowles created the Devon School, a fictionalized version of Phillips Exeter Academy, which Knowles had attended.

The coming-of-age novel centers on two school friends, Gene and Finny, and includes the death of Finny. Tobias Wolff's *Old School* (2003) is also set in a boarding school, which is probably based on the Hill School in Pennsylvania, which Wolff attended. He went on to become a university teacher, having studied at the University of Oxford and Stanford University, where he was appointed professor of English and creative writing in 1997. In *Old School*, the English teachers are portrayed as superior to all other subject teachers by virtue of the gift of literature that they can give to their pupils.

In the Australian novel *Picnic at Hanging Rock* (1967), Joan Lindsay creates an atmospheric account of a school outing by a group of girls from an exclusive boarding school in Victoria. Set in 1900, the novel is written as a true story, recounting how the girls mysteriously disappear while climbing Hanging Rock, in the Mount Macedon area.

The somewhat sinister headmistress Mrs. Appleyard tries to cope with the impact that the event has on the school. However, local concern escalates when some of the teachers either resign or meet with a tragic end, and pupils are withdrawn from the school. Later, we learn that Mrs. Appleyard's body was found at the foot of Hanging Rock. The novel was made into a very successful film in 1975, in which Rachel Roberts played Mrs. Appleyard.

Above:

Scene from the 1975 movie based on the 1967 novel Picnic at Hanging Rock, *showing headmistress Mrs. Appleyard (Rachel Roberts) and Miss McGraw (Vivean Gray).*

Above:

Poster for the movie Blue Murder at St. Trinian's *(1957), taken from the boarding school novels inspired by Ronald Searle's cartoons.*

TEACHERS IN NOVELS FOR CHILDREN

The genre of boarding-school fiction for children has been popular for well over a century. The Victorian novelist L. T. Meade set novels in girls' boarding schools, as did Angela Brazil in the early 20th century. The *Billy Bunter* stories by Charles Hamilton were set in the fictional Greyfriar's School for boys. The stories featured teachers such as Mr. Quelch, who was greatly feared by the boys.

The 1940s saw the creation of cartoons by Ronald Searle in which he developed characters modeled on schoolgirls he had observed in Cambridge. The cartoons eventually lead to the development of a series of *St. Trinian's* books and to several *St. Trinian's*

comedy films. At St. Trinian's, the school crest was a skull-and-crossbones. The schoolgirls were invariably portrayed as fearless, ink-stained jokers, while the teachers were recognizable stereotypes.

Many fictional teachers are to be found in the novels of Elinor Brent-Dyer and Enid Blyton. Brent-Dyer penned the *Chalet School* series of novels, while the very prolific Enid Blyton wrote a series of novels set in a school called Malory Towers and another series set in St. Clare's School. Elinor Brent-Dyer was a schoolteacher, but her own experience was of teaching in British day schools while her creation, called the Chalet School, was an exclusive boarding school in Switzerland.

Enid Blyton was also a teacher and taught at a small independent school for boys in Kent. She also worked as a private governess. However, her novels are based on imagination, and both Malory Towers and St. Clare's are boarding schools for middle and upper-middle class girls. The teachers are often stereotypes, such as the French mistresses Mamzelle Dupont and Mamzelle Rougier. Both series contain a popular headmistress. Miss Grayling, in Malory Towers, and Miss Theobald, in St. Clare's, are portrayed as model headteachers, who are strict but also fair to the pupils.

Today, perhaps the best-known fictional boarding school in the world is Hogwart's School of Witchcraft and Wizardry created by J.K. Rowling in the *Harry Potter* novels. The *Harry Potter* books have become the best-selling book series in history, and were the basis for a hugely successful series of films.

Rowling worked briefly as a teacher of English in Portugal and began to write fiction. The teachers in the *Harry Potter* novels are eccentric individuals with names such as Mad-Eye Moody, Quirinus Quirrell, Horace Slughorn, Severus Snape, and Pomona Sprout. Professor Minerva McGonagall and Headmaster Albus Dumbledore are the most influential teachers, leading the Hogwart's pupils by example.

Right:
Professor Snape (Alan Rickman) in the movie version of J.K. Rowling's novel Harry Potter and the Sorcerer's Stone *(1997).*

Teachers in the Movies

Teachers have featured in many cinema genres, from comedy to horror, musicals to film noir. More often than not, teachers are portrayed as heroes, saving youngsters from crime and poverty, and even from parents who fail to understand their offspring. Sometimes teachers emerge as romantic figures, while some films present teachers as cruel, unfeeling, and even sadistic. Hundreds of films have placed the teacher at the center of the action, and many have celebrated the lives of real teachers.

THE TEACHER AS HERO

Perhaps the most common way in which screenwriters have approached the task of portraying the lives of teachers is to see them as heroes. The 1955 movie *Blackboard Jungle* defined some of the features of the teacher-hero. In the movie, war veteran Rich Dadier (Glenn Ford) takes a teaching job in a tough New York high school. His greatest classroom challenge is the antisocial behavior of his pupils, especially that of Artie West (Vic Morrow) and Gregory

Miller, played by Sidney Poitier. Twelve years later, Poitier starred as teacher—Mr. Thackeray—in a strikingly similar movie, *To Sir, with Love* (1967). The film is set in a London inner-city school where academic successs is low, and racial tensions run high. Mr. Thackeray tries to win the trust of his pupils, inspiring them to make a success of their lives. The film closes as Thackeray, faced with grinding challenges, has to decide whether to leave the school and abandon teaching, or stay and battle on.

Right:
Sidney Poitier as Mr. Thackeray in To Sir, with Love *(1967), set in a troubled inner-city school.*

To Sir, with Love presents the teacher as an idealist who wants to challenge the cynicism and angst of a group of teenagers. The film positions the teacher in combat with tough pupils: the teacher only triumphs when he manages to "win over" the bad kids. The success of the teacher pivots on his ability to inspire his pupils, and be their hero. The "teacher as hero" is a theme to which many moviemakers return, giving us films such as *Conrack* (1974), *Teachers* (1984), *Stand and Deliver* (1988), *Lean on Me* (1989), and *Dangerous Minds* (1995). The movie climax is sometimes reached when pupils excel in a performance inspired by the hero-teacher, as seen in *Music of the Heart* (1999), *Take the Lead* (2006), and the *Sister Act* movies (1992, 1993).

Perhaps the best-known "teacher as hero" movie is *Dead Poets Society* (1989), in which Mr. Keating

(Robin Williams) returns to his old school to take up a post as English teacher. From his arrival, he is presented as a breath of fresh air in a school that is suffocated by ancient traditions. A series of scenes develop his image as a great liberator, who will give the boys intellectual freedom. His mantra is *carpe diem* (sieze the day), and he encourages his pupils to follow their dreams at any cost. His unusual teaching methods include getting the boys to stand on their desks, so they learn to understand what it is to see things from different perspectives. Poetry is taught while kicking soccer balls around, and rigid definitions are torn out of English textbooks.

Several pupils are deeply affected by his charismatic teaching, especially Todd Anderson (Ethan Hawke) and Neil Perry (Robert Sean Anderson). Mr. Keating's influence on Todd is a positive one, and he

learns to speak confidently and believe in himself. But for Neil, the consequences of Keating's idealism are devastating. Neil's father is determined his son will go to Harvard medical school. Neil, under Mr. Keating's influence, develops a passion for acting, and choses this as his future. Unable to cope with the vengeful anger of his father, Neil commits suicide. Blame for indirectly causing the suicide is placed on Mr. Keating, who is forced to resign his post. In a memorable moment, his devoted pupils climb silently onto their desks and salute their former teacher as he leaves.

THE INSPIRATIONAL TEACHER

When Keating, in *Dead Poets Society*, awakened a love of literature in his pupils, he did so by using innovative and original teaching methods. This is also the ruse adopted by a history teacher (Ryan Reynolds) in *School of Life* (2005), who arrives in a school determined to inspire his students. "Mr. D" becomes so popular that he is put in pole position to win the Teacher of the Year Award to the envy of rival staff member Mr. Warner.

Many other movies show how inspirational teachers can provoke the hostility of their colleagues and superiors. The award-winning French film *Les Choristes* (*The Chorus*, 2004) also presents the arrival of a new teacher in a hostile environment. Clément Mathieu (Gérard Jugnot) is a music teacher who takes a position at a grim boarding school where many of the boys are misfits. Despite opposition from his superiors, he manages to create a superb choir in which the talents of the boys can flourish.

While *Les Choristes* provides a serious treatment of the theme of the inspirational teacher who draws out the musical talents of his pupils, many other movies take this general plot and give it a comedic twist. In *Sister Act 2: Back in the Habit* (1993), for example, Sister Mary Clarence (Whoopi Goldberg) takes on a group of indifferent pupils in a rundown parochial school. The school is about to be closed down, but Sister Mary Clarence saves the day by creating a school choir that goes all the way to the finals of the choral state championships. The uplifting performances echo those that director Alan

Left:

Robin Williams as the inspirational teacher Mr. Keating in the film Dead Poets Society *(1989).*

"I am a teacher! I am a teacher first, last, always!"

The Prime of Miss Jean Brodie *(1969)*

Parker features in *Fame* (1980), a musical film set in the New York School for the Performing Arts, where the kids become superstars by the time the curtain goes up on the annual graduation show.

More recently, the triumph of the teacher and students via a musical performance is also featured in *Music of the Heart* (1999). Based on a true story, the film charts the struggles of violin teacher Roberta Guaspari (Meryl Streep) as she teaches in a Harlem school for underprivileged children. When their music program is closed down due to budget cuts, Roberta organizes a benefit concert at Carnegie Hall. Another movie based on a true incident concerning a teacher is *Schoolmaster Matsumoto* (1920). The film, which showed a teacher saving the life of a drowning child, became hugely popular in Japan and played nonstop for more than a year when it was first released. Six years later, it was still playing in cinemas.

While many of the inspirational teachers in movies are portrayed as likeable individuals, Maggie Smith's portrayal of the title role in *The Prime of Miss Jean Brodie* (1969) vividly created a completely eccentric teacher in inter-war Edinburgh. Like Mr. Keating in *Dead Poets Society*, Miss Brodie gathers a clique of devoted pupils around her. And like Mr. Keating, her unique teaching style and charismatic influence ultimately lead to her downfall. The school demands that she resign, but she leaves reminding everyone that she is "a teacher first, last, always."

TEACHERS AND ADDITIONAL NEEDS

While *Renaissance Man* (1994), which shows Danny DeVito teaching Army recruits who have some learning difficulties, is essentially a comedy, there are several serious cinematic treatments of teachers working with children and adults with additional needs. One of the best-known is *The Miracle Worker* (1962), in which Anne Bancroft portrayed Anne Sullivan, the teacher of deaf-blind Helen Keller. Helen's father brings Sullivan to live with the family,

and her teaching approach helps Helen to find a way to communicate with the world. The film, based on the life of Helen Adams Keller (1880-1968), also shows how Sullivan introduces Keller to activism and to public life, and it allowed Bancroft to reprise the role she had played in the play based on Sullivan's education of Keller.

The film *Children of a Lesser God* (1986) is also adapted from a stage play by Mark Medoff, and it features a hearing-speech teacher, played by William Hurt. The play, which opened on Broadway in 1980, won three Tony awards, while the film garnered an Oscar for deaf actress Marlee Matlin.

Above:

Gérard Jugnot as music teacher Clément Mathieu in French film Les Choristes, *or* The Chorus *(2004).*

Opposite:

Maggie Smith as inspirational teacher Miss Jean Brodie in The Prime of Miss Jean Brodie *(1969).*

Teachers on Television

Teachers have featured in dozens of television shows, made-for-television movies, and adaptations of novels. Educational life is also featured in fly-on-the-wall documentaries that chart experiences in schools, and add to our understanding of how they work. Television series that offer a realistic portrayal of schooling have proven particularly popular with teenage audiences.

MADE-FOR-TV MOVIES

Many movies made for television have featured teachers and schools. Although film critics can be dismissive of the genre, there have been some acclaimed made-for-TV movies featuring Hollywood stars. Sometimes these have been remakes of successful Hollywood films or theater plays. For example, Bette Davis starred as teacher Miss Moffatt in the original movie theater version of *The Corn is Green* (1945). The film was adapted from a play by Emlyn Williams, which first opened in London in 1938. The play enjoyed a long run on Broadway in 1940–41, and was revived on Broadway and in London's West End in the 1980s.

Director George Cukor made a new version of the movie for television in 1979, with Katharine Hepburn perfectly cast as the strong-willed teacher who sets up a school in a Welsh mining town in the late 19th century. When Moffatt discovers a particularly bright student, she encourages him to rise above many obstacles to pursue his education further.

Another Hollywood cinema classic *The Bells of St. Mary's* (1945), which starred Bing Crosby and Ingrid Bergman, was also remade for television. Released in 1959, it starred Claudette Colbert as a nun who tries to save a rundown New York school.

NORTH AMERICAN HISTORICAL DRAMAS

Teachers in 19th-century classrooms have been vividly portrayed in some well-regarded television series and films; these were often developed from autobiographies of the era. For generations of late 20th-century viewers, the one-room school and its surroundings seen in TV series like *Little House on the Prairie* provided a sense of what life was like for children and teachers on the American frontier in the 19th century and into the early 20th century.

Little House on the Prairie

Drawing on the autobiographical writing of Laura Ingalls Wilder (1867–1957), *Little House on the Prairie* was filmed for television between 1974–84. Laura Ingalls Wilder was raised in Wisconsin, Kansas, Minnesota, and South Dakota. In the television series, most of her childhood and education are located in a single setting—a small town called Walnut Grove.

Many scenes drew on Laura Ingalls Wilder's own experiences. She had become a teacher at the age of 16 in a one-room school in De Smet, South Dakota. Although she never graduated from high school, her own education prepared her to teach at the school and contribute to the family income. In the television series, young Laura (Melissa Gilbert) and her older sister, Mary (Melissa Sue Anderson), are excellent students. Mary, whose teaching career is abandoned when she loses her sight, marries a teacher at a school for the blind in Iowa. Laura marries Almanzo Wilder (Dean Butler), brother of her schoolteacher, Miss Eliza Jane Wilder (Lucy Lee Flippin). The drama portrays Miss Wilder as a caricature of 19th-century women teachers. Bespectacled and wearing her hair in a severe bun, she spends all of her spare time reading. When Laura takes over from Miss Eliza in the Walnut Grove school, she is a more relaxed teacher who communicates easily with her pupils.

Opposite:
Melissa Gilbert as Laura from the TV series Little House on the Prairie.

Anne of Green Gables

The "inspiring schoolmistress" character also features in the television and film adaptations of *Anne of Green Gables*, based on the autobiographical writing of L.M. Montgomery. Perhaps the best-known adaptation of the novel is the 1985 miniseries made by CBC, starring Megan Follows as Anne, a pupil at the local school in the fictional Avonlea, a town on Prince Edward Island, Canada. Inspired by the teaching of "kindred spirit" Miss Stacy (Marilyn Lightstone), Anne becomes top of her class in her final year and wins a scholarship to train as a teacher at Queen's College. She eventually returns to Avonlea to take over the local school from Miss Stacy.

The education of the fictional Anne is based on author Lucy Maude Montgomery's own life. Montgomery was raised in Cavendish, Prince Edward Island. She attended grade school there, and in 1893, she went to Prince of Wales College, Charlottetown, to train as a schoolteacher. She then attended Dalhousie University in Nova Scotia before working as a teacher in several schools.

The Waltons

The single-room schoolhouse and inspiring local schoolmistress also feature in the television series *The Waltons*, based on the book *Spencer's Mountain* by Earl Hamner Jr. Set in a fictional town in Virginia, most of the action spans the 1930s and 1940s, told in a series of stories set against a backdrop of the Depression and World War II. Miss Hunter (Mariclare Costello) is the local schoolmistress, teaching children of all ages, including the seven Waltons. It is she who encourages John-Boy (Richard Thomas) to pursue his love of writing, and he eventually goes to Boatwright College, a fictional college modeled on Richmond College (later part of the University of Virginia).

TEACHERS ON BRITISH TELEVISION

Many television series and made-for-television programs have featured schools and teachers. Some have been adaptations of well-known 19th-century novels by authors such as Charles Dickens, but there have also been several well-received series set in fictional modern schools. Television has also given

Right:
The Walton family from the TV series The Waltons, *which features the journey of John-Boy Walton from farm boy to a college student.*

scope to animators to create cartoon programs set in schools.

Dickens on Screen

The British 19th-century schoolroom has been vividly re-created in several television films and series. The novels of Charles Dickens, which have been adapted in more than 400 films and television series, have provided some of the most memorable teachers and schools on screen. In many versions of *Oliver Twist,* the world of the workhouse school is

re-created, while *Hard Times* gives a glimpse into a different type of education. *Oliver Twist* has been made into several TV miniseries, first in 1962, then later in 1999 and 2007. *Hard Times*, the novel in which Dickens attacked factory-like schools and demoralizing teaching was serialized for British television in 1977 and 1994. In *Hard Times*, Mr. Gradgrind is headmaster of a grim school in an English industrial town, appropriately named Coketown. The role of Gradgrind was played by Patrick Allen in the 1977 miniseries.

Above:

Actors Timothy West and Patrick Allen as Bounderby and cruel teacher Gradgrind from the series Hard Times, *based on the Charles Dickens novel.*

Above:

Teacher Tony Mitchell (Michael Percival) with pupils at Grange Hill from the 1970s British television series.

Grange Hill

The 1970s also saw the release of what would become one of the longest-running British television series. *Grange Hill*, a drama set in a fictional school, started in 1978 and ran for 30 years. The series was created by Phil Redmond, who also created popular "soap" drama series such as *Brookside* and *Hollyoaks*.

From the start, episodes were issue-driven, and there was a gritty realism to the treatment of themes such as heroin addition and knife crime. Filming took place in many different schools, including Kingsbury High School in North London and Holborn College in Hammersmith, London.

Many of the *Grange Hill* teachers had nicknames, such as "Hoppy" Hopwood, "Sooty" Sutcliffe, "Bullet" Baxter, and "Scruffy" McGuffy. One of the best-known staff members in the school was the Deputy Headmistress Mrs. McCluskley (Gwyneth Powell), who featured in episodes screened over a period of 10 years. Mr. "Bronco" Bronson (Michael Sheard) was perhaps the most feared teacher, and his rigid discipline struck terror into the pupils.

Skins

Teenage problems and social issues also drove the plot lines in *Skins*, a British television series filmed from 2008–2013. Set in Bristol and focusing on sixth form students, the show's name came from the name for the papers used in "roll-your-own" cigarettes. The teachers are portrayed as having the strengths and weaknesses common to all teachers—they struggle with some pupils, they inspire others, and they are often exhausted by the process.

TEACHERS AND TEEN TV

Several very popular Japanese television series for teens have been set in schools. *HanaYori Dango* was a teen drama series released in 2005. Set in a prestigious school, Eitoku Gakuen, the series covers issues such as bullying and teenage romance. A more light-hearted school series called *First Class* was released in Singapore between 2008 and 2009. In the series, teachers feature quite prominently, such as Gay Beh Song (Patrick Teoh), the irritable science teacher, and Noel Lee (Mark Zee), the vain PE teacher.

Successful teen movies have sometimes inspired the development of a television series. The cult teen movie *Clueless* (1995) was a huge success when it was released, grossing $56 million at the box office. The film is a loose reworking of the theme of Jane Austen's *Emma*, with Cherylin "Cher" Horowitz as the lead character, and high school romance, social networking, and matchmaking creating the action. A spin-off television series followed in 1996, continuing the story of the high school social scene. Well-known *Clueless* teachers include Mr. Hall and Miss Geist, who were "matchmade" by Cher.

ANIMATED SERIES

The beautifully illustrated *Madeline* books by Austrian author Ludwig Bemelmans have been reworked into a cartoon TV series. The action in the original storybook for children was set in a French boarding school, where Madeline and her friends are watched over by Miss Clavel. The book was adapted for television as early as 1960, and several television specials were subsequently released between 1993 and 2001.

A children's school is also at the center of *Recess*, an American animated television series produced between 1997–2001. Six fourth-grade pupils are central to the activity at Third Street Elementary School. The series inspired an animated film *Recess: School's Out* (2001), which was produced by Walt Disney Pictures. The animations of teachers typically draw on teacher stereotypes. Ms. Finster is authoritarian and does not want anyone to have fun, while Ms. Grotke is something of an eccentric hippy who is popular with the children.

Above:

Miss Geist (Twink Caplan) and pupil Cher Horowitz (Rachel Blanchard), from the 1996 miniseries Clueless.

Teachers on Stage

Many theater plays have explored relationships between teachers and their students, and the school has been the locus of activity in a number of very successful dramatic productions. While some of these plays were adapted for the screen, the original stage versions are regularly reprised by both professional and amateur actors, reminding us of their appeal to audiences around the world.

TEACHERS AND OPPORTUNITY

One of the best-known and influential plays about the effect of the teacher on a pupil is George Bernard Shaw's *Pygmalion* (1913). In the play, Shaw explored how education could provide a young girl with new opportunities, liberating her from the confines that her social class and poverty had imposed. This is a motif that has been reworked by many writers in both plays and novels. *Pygmalion* retains its status as a key work about the influence of a teacher, because of its timeless appeal. Shaw balances humor and cynicism, as the play shows how a phonetics professor tries to teach a Cockney flower-seller to pass as a duchess. The play was an instant success when it opened in 1913 in Vienna, and it played in both New York and London in 1914.

Right:
Rex Harrison as Professor Henry Higgins and Julie Andrews as his pupil Eliza Doolittle in the musical My Fair Lady.

In 1938, the play was adapted for the screen, and it starred Leslie Howard and Wendy Hiller. But the best-known film of the play is *My Fair Lady* (1964), with Audrey Hepburn as Eliza and Rex Harrison in the role of Professor Higgins. Rex Harrison had also played Higgins in the stage musical of the same name, opposite Julie Andrews in the role of Eliza. The play *Pygmalion* has also been made into a film several times.

While Julie Andrews was the pupil in the stage version of *My Fair Lady,* she was the teacher in *The Sound of Music* (1965), when the smash-hit musical was turned into a film. Based on a true story, the Broadway musical was written by the renowned duo Richard Rodgers and Oscar Hammerstein, and opened in 1959. It was based on the memoirs of Maria Von Trapp, who abandoned her plans to become a nun in order to be a governess to the seven Von Trapp children. She uses singing and music to teach them, and her effect on the children

is very positive. By the end of the show, Maria has become both teacher and mother to the children.

TEACHERS AND CONVENTION

Willy Russell's *Educating Rita* (1980) takes the broad theme of *Pygmalion* and explores the teacher-pupil relationship in a different context. The play was developed for two actors, and commissioned by the Royal Shakespeare Company. It premiered at The Warehouse (now the Donmar Warehouse), London, with Julie Walters in the title role—a role she reprised in the film version of *Educating Rita* (2000). The play explores the relationship between mature-student Rita and her English tutor, Dr. Frank Bryant (Michael Caine). While their relationship remains platonic, it nonetheless turns his life upside-down.

Rita's personal warmth and her enthusiasm for literature awakens in him an acute sense of his own failure to become a poet. He realizes that the language of literary criticism has come to bore him,

Above:

Connie Fisher as Maria Von Trapp in the musical The Sound of Music. *She is teaching the children a musical scale using the song* Do-Re-Mi. *This song is often used in music education by teachers today.*

while Rita's honest response to poetry makes him laugh. While the play presents some of the limitations of university education, with its conventions and snobbery, it also shows how Rita's university experience liberates her from a life that had failed to satisfy her, even though this liberation comes at the cost of her marriage. Rita rebels against the conventions of her class, turning away from her family and her husband so she can pursue learning. The play's message is ulitimately optimistic, and Rita's future opens before her as one that will be both challenging and rewarding.

Julie Walters also starred in another very successful treatment of the influence of teachers on the lives of their pupils, when she played a dance teacher in the film of the drama *Billy Elliot* (2000). Mrs. Wilkinson (Julie Walters) encourages young Billy to pursue his dream to be a ballet dancer against the vigorous oppostition presented by his father, a coalminer who does not understand why his son wants to dance. The film provided the basis for the stage hit *Billy Elliot: The Musical* (2005), with music and lyrics by Elton John. It premiered in London's West End in 2005, and is still playing there. It also opened on Broadway, scooping up 10 Tony Awards.

Another drama that enjoyed a long run in London and New York is the comedy *The History Boys* (2004), by Alan Bennett. Set in a northern England grammar school, the play follows a group of boys who are preparing for entrance examinations to Oxbridge. Three of their teachers are central to the drama: Irwin, Hector, and Lintott. Through the characters, Bennett manages to capture different "teacher types," but our sympathy is greatest for Hector, an older teacher who loves learning for its own sake. *The History Boys* was adapted as a film in 2006.

Left:

Douglas Hector (Richard Griffiths) and Mrs. Lintott (Frances de la Tour) with pupils, from The History Boys *at the Lyttleton Theater, 2005.*

Poetry and Teaching

Teachers and teaching have been celebrated in poetry for centuries. Many poets spent some of their professional lives as teachers, and the teaching of poetry in universities is vivified by the contribution of poets today. In Britain, "Poetry by Heart" is a competition that celebrates the pleasure of learning poetry, the equivalent to Poetry Out Loud in the United States.

TEACHER POETS

Many contemporary poets work as teachers, either in creative writing programs or in more general teaching roles in schools or universities. Several have written inspirational poems about teaching, including award-winning American poets Lucia Perillo and Mary Ruefle. Internationally famous past poets who served as teachers include:

Walt Whitman (1819–1892)

The 19th-century American author of *Leaves of Grass* worked as a teacher, journalist, and government clerk. In 1840–1841, Whitman published a series of 10 newspaper editorials called *Sun-Down Papers—From the Desk of a Schoolmaster*. His poetry has been hugely influential on later American poets, and Ezra Pound said of him: "America's poet ... He is America."

Stephane Mallarme (1842–1898)

A leading French poetry prize is named after the influential symbolist poet Stephane Mallarme, who worked as an English teacher throughout his life and had a modest income. He held salons at his Paris home to discuss poetry, art, and philosophy, and was acquainted with an intellectual circle that included writers such as W.B.Yeats, Rainer Maria Rilke, Paul Valéry, and Paul Verlaine; artists like Claude Monet and James McNeill Whistler; and musicians such as Claude Debussy.

Seamus Heaney (1939–2013)

The Nobel Prize winning Irish poet Seamus Heaney studied English at Queen's University, Belfast, before going to St. Joseph's Teacher Training College, where he later became a lecturer. In 1966, he began lecturing at Queen's University, Belfast. His first book, *Eleven Poems*, was published in 1965. In addition to writing many volumes of poetry, Heaney had a distinguished teaching career, lecturing at the University of California, Berkeley, and at Harvard University, and he was elected Professor of Poetry at the University of Oxford in 1989. He received the Nobel Prize for Literature in 1995.

From left to right:

Teacher poets and Nobel Prize for Literature winners Seamus Heaney, Gabriela Mistral, DerekWalcott, and Wole Soyinkawe.

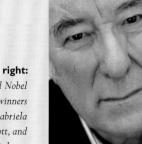

Above left:

American poet Walt Whitman worked intermittently as a teacher.

Above right:

19th-century African-American poet Frances Harper (1825–1911) was a political campaigner for the abolition of slavery and the first woman to teach sewing at the Union Seminary, a work-study school operated by the African Methodist Episcopal Church near Columbus, Ohio.

Left:

Portrait in oil of French symbolist poet and teacher Stephane Mallarme by Edouard Manet (1876).

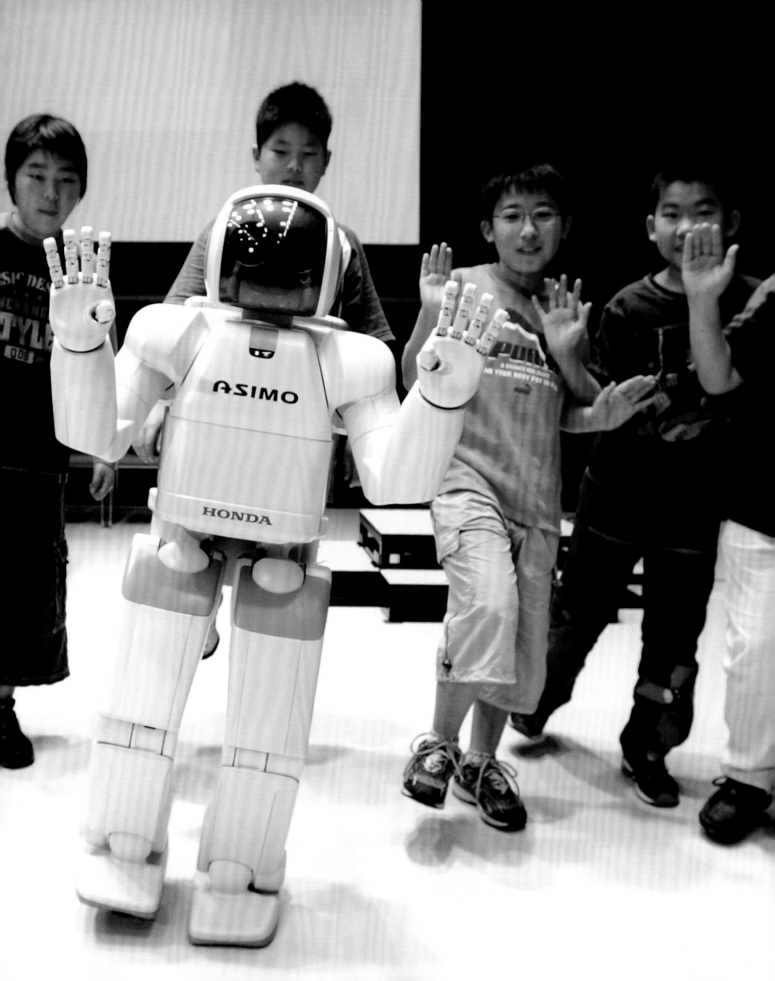

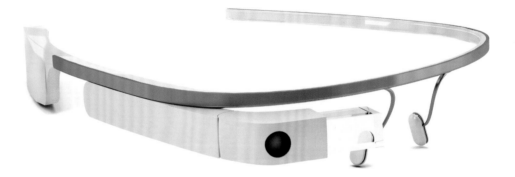

4 TEACHING TODAY AND TOMORROW

Teachers in the 21st century stand on the shoulders of the giants of educational theory and pedagogy of previous centuries while also enjoying the innovations that have accompanied the technological revolution. The classroom has become a creative learning space, networked to the world via the Internet.

Teachers and Educational Innovation

Education policy drives much educational change, but teachers are also change agents. While they have to work with requirements such as syllabi and curricula, they are at the chalkboard, and they know what changes and innovations are really needed in their schools and classrooms. Teachers are involved in many programs to support schools, innovate in learning, and prepare children to deal with ongoing rapid change in areas such as technology and communications.

TEACH FOR AMERICA

To respond to the demands to raise school standards in the United States, schools need a constant supply of motivated, well-educated teachers who are willing to work in all kinds of schools, including those in low-income communities that are experiencing challenges. Many local and national projects have been established to support such schools and widen opportunities for the students.

One such program is Teach For America, established in 1989. Its purpose was to respond to the fact that there are more than 16 million children growing up in poverty in the United States, a third

Right:
A Teach For America corps member provides focused feedback for a student.

Opposite:
Teach For America prepares highly motivated graduates to work in schools throughout the United States, including schools experiencing challenges.

of whom won't complete high school, and the majority of whom will never graduate from college. Teach For America's founder Wendy Kopp had an idea to link high-achieving college graduates with high-need schools. She developed the concept of a not-for-profit teaching "corps," where graduates would commit to teach for two years.

Teach For America provides training and support, and places corps members in partner schools across America. Susan Asiyanbi, executive vice president of program continuum, knows there are many reasons young graduates are attracted to joining the Teach For America corps. "If you were to ask any of our corps members what compelled them to join this work, each one would give you a slightly different reason or story," Asiyanbi explains. "However, what we find to be the common thread linking all of these reasons together is an innate desire to be a

"In the past four years, I have worked with a number of corps members and alumni teachers. Each of them brings their own experiences into our building and they all share a deep-rooted passion for our kids. It seems that there is no challenge too great for their determination."

Carole Wilson Frye

Principal, Clarence Farrington School, Indianapolis

part of something bigger and the belief that solving educational equity is possible in their lifetime."

Graduates who are looking for something that gives some meaning and direction to their lives are often attracted by the change to join this vibrant teaching corps. "It is incredibly challenging and humbling, and calls on those who choose to join the movement for educational equity (in and outside the classroom) to stare down injustice, give their best every day, and to push themselves to grow, get better, and learn from the parents and community members we serve," says Asiyanbi.

Over its 25-year history, Teach For America has trained more than 50,000 leaders, many of whom had not previously considered going into education, to become teachers in urban and rural low-income communities across the nation. Asiyanbi explains that Teach For America "deeply values data as one tool for improving our approach and identifying best practices." She refers to the growing body of rigorous research, including recent studies by Mathematica and RAND, which indicate that Teach For America teachers have a positive impact on student learning. "Tennessee, Louisiana, and North Carolina have each studied the effectiveness of beginning teachers from local teacher preparation programs, and all three have identified Teach For America as one of the most effective teacher providers," Asiyanbi advises. "Corps members see themselves as partners in our communities, schools and across districts with a shared goal of expanding educational opportunities for all students. As we continue to work toward stronger supports and training for educators in our highest-need schools alongside our partners in communities, schools and across districts, we are eager to use data to continue to do just that."

Selecting the right graduates to join this teaching corps is important because Teach For America's aim is to have a diverse range of talents and skills and provide good role models for children. Individuals of all backgrounds gain admission to the Teach For America corps. "A diverse teaching force brings a wide range of excellent education," Asiyanbi says. "At the same time, since educational inequity in our country is largely drawn along lines of race and class, we know that it's particularly important to foster the leadership of individuals who share the racial and economic backgrounds of our students."

"I will always remember the four years that Mr. Vargas, who entered teaching through Teach For America, changed my life. Before stepping into his classroom, I had developed a strong dislike—a strong dislike for the school system, but I loved learning... Stepping into his classroom every day and hearing lessons from Mr. Vargas was an escape from the trauma I faced outside of the school. Vargas taught me that there was so much more in this world than what I was offered."

Clifton Kinnie

Former student of Michal Vargas, St. Louis '09 corps member, and current freshman at Howard University

One of the greatest challenges in high-need schools is the high rate of teacher turnover. Reflecting on this problem, Susan Asiyanbi acknowledges, "Nearly half of all teachers leave the classroom within five years, and in high-need schools the rate is even higher."

But the team at Teach For America is optimistic. "We believe more can be done to keep effective teachers in under-resourced schools and hard-to-staff positions, no matter which path they've taken to the classroom," she continues.

And there is cause for optimism. Two-thirds of the teaching corps alumni continue to work in educa-tion, and 30 percent remain in the classroom. "The Teach For America network includes more than 50,000 corps members, alumni, and staff members … our alumni are taking on a wide range of leader-ship roles that reflect their diverse perspectives and experiences," says Asiyanbi, and she continues: "As a part of our theory of how to facilitate systemic change in low-income communities, we know that we need our corps members, who have had incredible experiences working with students in low-income areas, to enter into other fields to continue to affect change." Asiyanbi concludes with pride: "These deeply impassioned individuals are our legacy and our greatest contribution to the American education system."

Above:

In addition to recruiting excellent graduates, Teach For America aims to provide strong role models for young people.

Teachers as Life Changers

There are countless teachers and educators who work for children, youths, and adults outside the mainstream school system. Tireless in their commitment to share the joys of learning, they help their students to manage physical, economic, and social challenges.

"My course was changed and set from that moment in fourth grade when a teacher decided to take matters into his own hands."

Luis A. Ubinãs

Some teachers change their students' lives by taking courageous steps. Luis A. Ubinãs, former president of the Ford Foundation, has told of the extraordinary lengths to which one teacher went on his behalf. Ubinãs grew up poor in the Bronx, supported by his mother who worked in a sweatshop and by his grandmother. Like many Hispanic families in New York in the 1970s and '80s, his family valued education. But Ubinãs struggled at school, and they could not figure out why this was the case. Then one of his teachers spotted that Ubinãs was very gifted, but bored by lessons. The teacher decided to take matters into his own hands, as Ubinãs recounts in Arlene Alda's *Just Kids from the Bronx*:

"He personally took me to the Bank Street School, Allen-Stevenson School, and St. Bernard's—all private schools in Manhattan. He took me out of school, took me by the hand, bought me subway tokens, bought me lunch … Miraculously, I was accepted in all three schools … From Allen-Stevenson I went to Collegiate, and from there to Harvard and then to Harvard Business School."

Wormwood Scrubs Pony Center, London

People who have made a huge difference to the lives of others through voluntary education initiatives are also acknowledged. Britain showed its appreciation to Mary Joy Langdon by inviting her to carry the Olympic Torch as it was relayed to its position for the 2012 Olympics.

Mary Joy is a Catholic sister, but as newspapers have reported, she is no ordinary nun. Way back in the 1970s, Mary Joy was Britain's first-ever female firefighter, and she has also hiked mountains and rapelled down buildings—invariably to raise

money to improve the lives of children. Mary Joy is an accomplished horsewoman, and her talents were put to great use in 1989 when she was offered the use of some scrubland and three ponies. She set about establishing the Wormwood Scrubs Pony Center in urban west London. "It was never a pre-planned idea," Langdon says. "It just developed from opportunities and circumstances." Langdon had the idea to use the ponies to set up an inner-city community riding school, which would welcome children with learning difficulties and physical disabilities, and teach them to ride. The help of some volunteers and a lot of hard work resulted in the school getting off the ground in 1989, offering groundbreaking equine therapy and education.

In 1994, the Center attracted the attention of the television series *Challenge Anneka*, which helped to raise much-needed funds to build an indoor arena.

The center also attracted the attention of the artist Lucian Freud, who stopped by one day to see if he could paint one of the horses. A great friendship grew between Freud and the voluntary teachers at the Center, as the artist worked on portraits of a mare called Sioux. The resulting painting now hangs at Chatsworth House.

"Equine therapy is so beneficial for these youngsters. They become one with the horse enabling them to leave their difficulties and troubles behind."

Mary Joy Langdon, IJS

Wormwood Scrubs Pony Center

The Center has gone from strength to strength, and children are offered the chance to develop a range of skills. Not all the children can ride, but as Mary Joy Langdon explains, all can achieve success. "All the children that attend are given the opportunity to become achievers. For children who have been poor achievers, this can be very positive and can lead them on to developing other skills. The ponies become a catalyst for learning." The children learn a range of subjects related to horses, which Langdon outlined. These include anatomy, first aid, fire safety, poetry, public speaking, wild life, farming, saddlery, health and safety, security, road safety, rider nutrition, understanding training, and pony math.

Learning to care for the ponies develops a sense of responsibility in the children. "The children also learn how to take a pride in what they are doing and in their own personal turnout. For example, they have to learn how to polish their boots. One mother said that on school days, her daughter needed a great deal of help in dressing but on Saturdays, she manages to dress herself correctly," Langdon explains.

There are countless success stories attached to Wormwood Scrubs Pony Center. Most reflect the ability of children to respond to the horses and rise to great challenges. Mary Joy recounted the achievements of one young girl who attends a Special School on four school days a week, and attends the Pony Center on the fifth day. "Since she has been doing this, her academic schoolwork has greatly improved. At the Pony Center, she is learning vocational skills that will give her a head start into adulthood. She is also following a recognized program, adapted to be associated with horses … and she is following a basic science course, which is also equine-adapted," says Langdon.

Other children with profound disabilities have learned to count by doing activities that required them to say, "One, two, three, walk on. One, two, three, halt." And one little boy, who had never picked up a paintbrush, became absorbed in a "Paint Pony" class, using a sponge brush to paint on the side of a real pony. Langdon also talks animatedly of the learning activities that include children sitting contentedly on ponies in front of a giant mirror, as they learn to imitate actions and develop coordination.

A high point for the students was welcoming celebrity Clare Balding to launch the Center's first pony simulator in 2015. This electronic horse is now being used in education and training. The extraordinary work being done by Langdon and her fellow volunteer teachers has captured the attention of Princess Anne, who paid a special visit to the Center in 2014. And in 2015, the Center was awarded the Queen's Award for Voluntary Service, which is the equivalent of a group MBE, or Member of the British Empire, an appointment that acknowledges exceptional contributions to charitable efforts, public service, and the arts and sciences.

The Clemente Program

When the 2014 National Humanities Medal was awarded to the Clemente Course in the Humanities (CCH), it acknowledged the tireless efforts of teachers who believe that humanities education

"Day after day, you created an atmosphere of academic excellence and warm welcome. I could never figure out how you did it; I could just observe the results in every class. I know I speak for the entire class when I say 'Thank you so very much. Thank you.'"

L.D.

Halifax Clemente Humanities 101, Class of 2011

should be available to everyone, including those who have been denied cultural, social, and economic opportunities.

The Clemente Course in the Humanities runs in 20 U.S. cities, and in Korea, Australia, and Canada, and was founded in 1995 by Earl Shorris, social critic and author of *The Art of Freedom: Teaching Humanities to the Poor*. Named for Roberto Clemente, the American All-Stars baseball player and champion of charitable work in Latin American and Caribbean countries, the program provides free, accredited courses in the humanities throughout the United States. This opens the possibility of further college education to people who are marginalized by economic or personal circumstances, empowering them with the means to improve their own lives.

One student of philosophy at the CCH in Harlem described the program as "a monument to the virtue of humanism. At first glance we are simply a room of people sitting in a box, but if you ask any of us in the most honest of words what it is we do, we learn, we think, and we write."

A distinctive feature of Clemente courses is that the teachers are exceptionally dedicated and very well-regarded by their students. At the Boston Clemente program, as students gathered for the first class of the term in September in a cheerful Dorchester hall, they reflected on what they consider to be the characteristics of a "good teacher." Passion, dedication, patience, and kindness are what the students respect in teachers. They agreed that some of their best teachers have been family members who helped them to believe in the value of education. One student shared that her father back in Trinidad used to say, "I will boil those books and make you drink it." He inspired her to pursue learning, just as her young son now inspires her, and—in many ways—teaches her new things.

Deeply reflective about the teaching profession, the Clemente students have also known schoolteachers who had high expectations for them and who were good role models. Students agreed that teaching is a vocation, and that a good teacher will do more than

"To the Clemente Course in the Humanities, for improving the lives of disadvantaged adults. The Clemente Course has brought free humanities education to thousands of men and women, enriching their lives and broadening their horizons."
White House Citation, 2014

deliver a curriculum: "they will embrace it with love, enthusiasm, and vigor."

Having decided to return to education, the students who gathered in that Dorchester classroom on a damp fall evening as darkness fell outside knew that they were about to embark on something that would be a life-changer. If they succeed in the four Clemente humanities modules, they get credits from the prestigious Bard College. The English literature module is taught by Professor Ann Murphy, who says that even if students don't manage to complete the course, it is still "absolutely a life-changer ... they find they are transformed by the experience."

Murphy, an English professor from Assumption College, has contributed evening classes to the Clemente program for several years, along with Professors from several other New England universities, including Boston College and Harvard. She says that the students really relish "the chance to talk about books and ideas—things that middle-class college students take for granted." She finds the Clemente students are usually a little older than college undergraduates, and this is a strength. "They are so engaged," Murphy says. "They don't see their studies as an entitlement, but as a privilege. They respond to literature with reflection and maturity. Their life experiences help them to make meaning from their studies."

Below:

Teacher Jonas Baston, a winner of the Bravo award for arts education, uses drama as a method for teaching classroom lessons. Here, he is working with students at a school in Pacific Palisades, CA.

Teachers and the Arts

Innovation in teaching is not only the preserve of technologists: many teachers working in the area of the arts have made unique contributions to teaching. They have also changed peoples' lives, showing exceptional faith in their students.

DRAMA TEACHING

Actor Al Pacino credits his drama teacher has having changed the entire course of his life. Raised by his grandmother in the Bronx, Pacino was doing poorly in school, but showed talent at acting:

"There was this teacher, Blanch Rothstein, the drama teacher, who went to my apartment to talk to my grandmother and to tell her things about me. To this day I don't know what they were, but I think they had to do with encouraging me to be an actor. She actually climbed those five flights of stairs to say that to my grandmother.

This is why to this day, I say, 'It's the teachers!' That's why when anybody says 'teacher,' I light up. There it was, in this South Bronx public school, recognizing something I was doing that made her say that there was real hope there."
Al Pacino, in Arlene Alda's *Just Kids From the Bronx*.

Drama teachers such as Konstantin Stanislavsky and Lee Strasberg have been innovators in the field, developing techniques that acting students study. Conservatories of drama, such as the Royal Academy of Dramatic Art (RADA) in London and Julliard College in New York, prepare their students for degrees in acting, and their teachers work on areas such as movement, voice, techniques, and theater history.

Studying the history of an artistic discipline is valued as highly as studying techniques and skills. In colleges of music, drama, and art, teachers bring a depth of academic understanding to professional and practical training.

The influence of a great drama teacher does not end once the student graduates from college or

"Lee's great gifts are teaching and inspirational guidance…"

Cheryl Crawford

Producer/director on Lee Strasberg.

becomes successful. Many well-known actors rely on their drama teachers to advise them, and give them feedback on performances. The Oscar-winning British actor Eddie Redmayne still takes tips from his school drama teacher. He has said that he had "the greatest drama teacher … I continue to seek out his advice and work with him if I think I could use some feedback when I am preparing for a role." Redmayne won an Oscar for his portrayal of Stephen Hawking in *The Theory of Everything*, and received rave reviews for his performance in *The Danish Girl*. Tom Hanks also acknowledged the influence of his high school drama teacher when collecting his Oscar for his performance in *Philadelphia*: "… he showed that work in theater is an art, a life that can be pursued."

Above:

Innovative drama teacher Lee Strasberg working with Al Pacino on The Godfather, *1974.*

VISUAL ARTS TEACHING

At the National College of Art and Design in Ireland, Fiona Loughnane teaches visual culture, which draws on her own studies in fine art and art history. She is passionate about her teaching and about ensuring that teaching is underpinned by research.

Like many teachers, Loughnane had an inspirational teacher when she was a student. The sculptor and teacher Lochlann O'Hoare influenced her work, and while she found him to be very demanding and often a harsh critic, he made her feel that her work was valuable. His teaching influenced Loughnane to pursue a career as a lecturer and researcher in Visual culture, working with undergraduate and postgraduate students. She describes her teaching style as very open; she likes to facilitate a lot of discussion and encourage her students to "discuss images and text in a critical way." She tries to give constructive comments on her students' work, though she knows she has high standards.

Like many Art college teachers, Loughnane is aware of the relatively poor visual awareness of many young people, and of the need for lecturers and teachers to be innovative. "Despite the dramatic increase in the circulation of images in a digital age, despite the role visual culture plays in the formation of their identities, few students have had any sustained engagement with the subject prior to college," she says. This means that her teaching must not only inspire students to become aware of the

Below:

A pupil and teacher in discussion in an art class.

"Every child is an artist. The problem is how to remain an artist once we grow up."

Pablo Picasso

power of images, but must also teach them how to be critical thinkers. She concludes, "My key aim is to get students to think critically about images, to interrogate the visual practices they study, the texts they read, and their own biases and judgments."

FAMOUS ART TEACHERS

Many artists have been inspiring art teachers. The Russian-French artist Marc Chagall (1887–1985) taught art at a Jewish boys' shelter in Russia for a year. And the mother of American modernism Georgia O'Keeffe (1887–1986) taught drawing for two years in the public school system in Texas

between 1912–14. She then went to Teachers College at Columbia University, and subsequently taught at Columbia College, South Carolina. O'Keeffe became head of art at West Texas State College in 1916. Pop-artist Corita Kent (1918–86), whose civil rights posters and antiwar murals are known throughout the United States, was a teacher at the Immaculate Heart College in Los Angeles, where she later became chair of the art department. Harlem painter and textile artist Faith Ringold (1930–) taught in the New York City public school system before teaching at college level. She is a professor emeritus of the University of California.

Above:

Tatiana Shapovalova, the leader of the Russian drawing school "Look," teaches children in the City Palace of Children's and Junior Arts, offering hobby circles for kids.

Teachers, Technology, and Change

With rapid changes in social media and technology, computer scientists and designers are working with teachers to harness digital resources for education purposes. The growth of online learning and MOOCs (massive open online courses) means the classroom has been reinvented as a virtual space. The teacher can connect with students remotely and can conduct online classes that bring people together from several countries.

Below:
Microsoft founder Bill Gates.

"Technology is just a tool. In terms of getting the kids working together and motivating them, the teacher is the most important."

Bill Gates

Some teachers feel that online learning makes teachers almost redundant, but most educators recognize the teacher is central to the experience of schooling—both online and in real time.

GAMING AND EDUCATION

By using the tools of technology, designers can create games and virtual worlds that support teachers. Dr. Wanda Gregory is director of the Center for Serious Play at the University of Washington, and she has worked with industry partners to develop the use of technology and games in both learning and health contexts. Her work has included a long period as senior director/ executive producer at HASBRO and Wizards of the Coast, and she also worked with Microsoft during the development stages of Xbox. She considers that while technological tools and "gamification" have a real place in schooling, it is "too early to predict the direct and measurable outcomes" of innovations in these areas.

Gregory knows many parents and teachers use what is known as "edutainment," or learning games and toys, especially with younger children. Some of the games are excellent, but Gregory does not believe they can replace the teacher. Instead, she says that "the win-win is for teachers to use interactive media to create curiosity ... to open doors." She also believes that teachers can make use of games and online learning to increase pupil's understanding. However, even then she asserts that the teacher is still needed to play a crucial role in managing the whole learning situation.

In schools, doing some online research is of very little lasting use to students, unless the teacher has planned for situations where the students will write critically about this research, Gregory suggests. Gregory teaches interactive media and entrepreneurship, and works on the applied use of games in education. Like many researchers who are also teachers, she remains convinced of the central role of the teacher in the educational experience.

Above:

The emergence of the MOOCs (massive open online courses) means that once they have a computer and Internet access, students can now avail themselves of online teaching provided by many universities.

The Museum as Teacher

Teachers have been involved in the creation and design of education museums and museums for children. Teachers recognize that the museum of today is a potent source of education, and museums have responded by devising exhibitions and learning activities that support different types of school curricula.

THE FIRST EDUCATIONAL MUSEUM

Founded in 1899, Brooklyn Children's Museum was the first institution of its kind. It was founded to educate urban children in natural science, but it expanded to include culture and technology. In the 1930s, it was supported by the Works Projects Administration, a New Deal agency employing millions of people to carry out public projects. As a result, the Brooklyn Children's Museum thrived during the Great Depression and had been visited by more than 9 million people by 1939.

By 1913, Boston's Science Teachers' Bureau, together with the Women's Education Association, had generated enough support to open the Boston Children's Museum. Their aim was to provide "… natural objects, books, pictures, charts, lantern slides, etc., whatever else is helpful in the science work of the Grammar, High and Normal Schools." Exhibits were arranged at children's eye level, and included shells, minerals, and birds. To expand the benefits of museum education, branch museums were located in schools in East and South Boston.

Rigjht:
At the Boston Children's Museum, interactive learning allows children to develop their understanding of science.

Under the direction of Michael Spock, son of Dr. Benjamin Spock, the museum was innovative in the area of hands-on learning, developing interactive exhibits. One of the permanent installations is a model kindergarten classroom, where children and parents can ask teachers questions about kindergarten education. The Japanese House is a popular zone in the museum where visitors can learn about Japanese culture.

MUSEUMS AND TEACHERS

In London, the V&A Museum of Childhood engages with teachers and pupils from elementary and secondary schools and complements the curriculum with teaching sessions. Children can also learn the skills of the museum curator and are taught how to identify different kinds of materials and designs, and how to create chronological frameworks. Because some children with additional learning needs may prefer a quieter environment in which to explore

activities and interactive tools, the museum hosts "quiet days" and provides short teaching sessions for children. The museum also delivers sessions to London Hospital Schools.

Japan's Hamada Children's Museum of Art also works with teachers, and supports school curricula. It runs a "Museum School" program where teachers and children can examine artworks and then work on collaborative creative projects.

Australia has paved the way for universities to become involved in museum education for children. At the University of Wollongong, the Early Start Discovery Space was launched in 2015, providing interactive experiences that are mapped to the syllabus of the New South Wales Board of Studies. Children learn to helm a ship and navigate a journey, or take a guided tour inside a giant inflatable "tummy" to see how digestion takes place.

Above:

At the Canadian Children's Museum in Quebec, educational experiences are provided to teach children about world travel. Here, children are riding on the museum's Pakistani bus.

Celebrating Teachers

All over the world each year, awards are made in recognition of the contribution of teachers to the education and personal development of children, youths, and adults, and there is now an international Teachers' Day, on October 5.

UNITED NATIONS WORLD TEACHERS' DAY

In 1994, the first World Teachers' Day was held on October 5 to mark the contribution of teachers all over the world. On that date each year, events and conferences are held around the world to celebrate teachers. Organizations and trade unions in many countries support the celebration, including in Japan, the United Kingdom, New Zealand, India, the United States, Canada, and Australia. UNESCO encourages celebratory events to mark the work of teachers, and to highlight the need to empower teachers to make a critical contribution to the UNESCO goals of universal education by 2020 and to eliminate gender disparities in education.

Some countries have adopted a different date for their Teachers' Day to mark the contribution of a national figure in education. In India, for example, Teachers' Day is on September 5 to mark the birth date of Sarvepalli Radhakrishnan, the philosopher and scholar who was India's president from 1962 to 1967.

Below:

School children pray and offer flowers to the portrait of Sarvepalli Radhakrishnan during the Teachers' Day celebration in Allahabad, India.

AWARDS FOR TEACHERS

In the United States, the National Teacher of the Year (NTOY) program was launched in 1952, and it is the oldest national honors program that focuses on excellence on teaching. A national committee selects the National Teacher of the Year from among the State Teachers of the Year. The NTOY must demonstrate exceptional dedication and be an inspiring teacher who has the respect and admiration of students, parents, and colleagues.

In India, the National Awards to Teachers were instituted in 1958. There are 374 awards, and each state, union, territory, or organization has a quota based on its number of teachers. Special awards are also made for teachers who promote inclusive education, and for teachers working with children who have disabilities. The awards ceremony takes place on Teachers' Day, September 5, each year. The Central Board of Secondary Education, India, also presents annual awards.

In Australia, the Australian Scholarships Group (ASG) presents annual awards to teachers. It sponsors the National Excellence in Teaching Awards, giving communities the opportunity to show their appreciation for inspirational principals and teachers. Deb Derrick, who won an award in 2014, has said the demands on teachers have increased, as they have more committee work, more contact with parents, and more technology and subjects to accommodate. However, she says teachers continue to take their jobs very seriously and care deeply about their students.

Sports teachers, and especially professional coaches, are also presented with awards. The BBC Sports Personality of the Year Coach Award has recognized sports coaches from all over the globe. Enzo Calzaghe has won the BBC Coach Award for training his son, boxer Joe Calzaghe, and he has also been awarded an MBE. The British cycling coach David John Brailsford CBE has also won the BBC Coach Award.

Teachers have also been given awards by their own states or communities, to acknowledge their excep-

Above:

Steve Ritz and the Green Bronx Machine project provide education in sustainable living and food production.

tional service. In 2011, Mexican schoolteacher Martha Rivera Alanis was given a special award for courage by the state governor. Alanis kept calm and took care of 15 children when a gunfight broke out a block away from the Monterrey school where she worked. To distract the children from the sounds of the gunfire, she encouraged them to lie down on the floor and then led them in songs.

In New York City, teacher Stephen Ritz has received an award for his work with pupils, which has included installing gardens. A teacher at Public School 55 in the South Bronx, Ritz's ideas for urban renewal and food production have had a remarkable effect on the school students, and he has started a health and wellness center based there called Green Bronx Machine.

"Better than a thousand days of diligent study is one day with a great teacher."

Japanese Proverb

Champions of Education

Many well-known public figures worked as teachers. Writers, actors, politicians, and famous athletes have all contributed to the education profession. Some continued to teach even when they had become celebrities, while others became supporters of the work of current educators.

Many teachers who became public figures have demonstrated a commitment not only to the education of youths, but also to supporting teachers. They have championed the teaching profession, showing gratitude to educators worldwide.

Maya Angelou (1928–2014)

When teacher and writer Maya Angelou died at 86, there were countless tributes to her extraordinary power to communicate with her students at Wake Forest University in North Carolina. She said of herself, "I am not a writer who teaches. I am a teacher who writes." She taught poetry, Shakespeare, and many courses that examined issues of race and politics. In her classes, she encouraged students to express opinions, saying, "You can say anything … The only thing is to defend it, and not be in love with any position, but to be in love with the search for truth."

David Putnam (1941–)

Distinguished filmmaker David Putnam is a champion of education innovation. Putnam retired from film production in the late 1990s to concentrate on initiatives in education and environmental protection. In 1998, he founded the National Teaching Awards for the U.K., and he was also chair of the National Film and Television School. He is a patron of the Shakespeare Schools Festival (SSF), which is the U.K.'s largest youth drama festival. Participants in the SSF perform abridged version of Shakespeare, and the Festival has worked with 4,842 teacher-directors since its inception in 2000. Novelist and former teacher Philip Pullman is also a patron.

J.K. Rowling (1965–)

While writing her best-selling novel *Harry Potter and the Sorcerer's Stone*, Rowling worked for a short while as an English teacher in Portugal. Although she left teaching and became a hugely successful author, she did not lose interest in education, and is a supporter of the Shannon Trust, a Scottish charity founded by Christopher Morgan in 1997 to teach reading in prisons. Morgan has developed a reading program and a peer-mentoring network to teach adults and young people to read, and his work has resulted in raised self-esteem and improved behavior in prisons.

From left to right:

British novelists and former teachers J.K. Rowling and Philip Pullman; Pakistani Nobel laureate Malala Yousafzai, who has championed women's education; U.S. Olympic bobsled gold medalist Steve Mesler, cofounder and president of Classroom Champions, a nonprofit that brings the advice of Olympians, Paralympians, and sports mentors into classrooms.

Left:
Pupils perform at the Shakespeare Schools Festival.

Below left:
Filmmaker David Putnam is a patron of the Shakespeare School Festival, founder of the U.K. National Teaching Awards, and a former chair of the National Film and Television School.

Below:
Maya Angelou told her young audience at the 1985 commencements to "dare to love … dare to care … dare to want to be significant and to admit it."

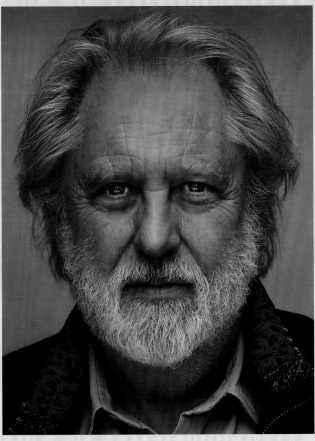

"Don't just teach because that's all you can do, teach because it's your calling."

Maya Angelou

Bibliography

BOOKS AND ARTICLES

Ade Ajayi, J.F. *General History of Africa*, Vol. 6. UNESCO/J. Curry, 1998.

Alda, Arlene. *Just Kids from the Bronx: Telling it the Way it Was.* NY: Holt & Co., 2015.

Alexander, Kristine 'Education during the First World War' www.wartimecanada. ca/essay/learning/education-during-first-world-war Accessed 4 November 2015.

Brown, Hubert O. 'Teachers and Teaching', in A. Postiglione and Wing On Lee, *Schooling in Hong Kong*. Hong Kong: Hong Kong University Press, 1998.

Burke, Catherine. *A Life in Education and Architecture: Mary Beaumont Medd*. London: Ashgate, 2013.

Clegg, Luther Bryan (ed.). *The Empty Schoolhouse: Memories of One-Room Texas Schools*. Texas: Texas A&M University Press, 1997.

Dalton, Mary M. *The Hollywood Curriculum: Teachers in the Movies*. NY and Oxford: Peter Lang, 2004.

Dewey, J. *Democracy and education: An introduction to the philosophy of education* (First published: 1916).

Else, Anne. *Listen to the Teacher: An Oral History of Women Who Taught in New Zealand, 1925–1945*. The Society, 1986.

Enss, Chris. *Frontier Teachers*. Connecticut and Montana: Morris Book Publishing, 2008.

Grant, Edward. *God and Reason in the Middle Ages*. Cambridge: Cambridge University Press, 2001.

Guthrie, James M. *Encyclopedia of Education*, Vols 1–8. New York: Macmillan, 2003.

Harrington, Joel. *The Unwanted Child: the Fate of Foundlings, Orphans and Juvenile Criminals in Early Modern Germany*. USA: University of Chicago Press, 2009.

Himola, Antti. 'The Sloyd Teachers' Working Methods in Finnish Comprehensive Schools.' *Procedia–Social and Behavioral Sciences*. Vol 45, 2012, pp. 41–53. Available at www.sciencedirect.com/science/article/pii/S187704281202277X Accessed 6 Nov 2015.

Maynes, Mary Jo. *Schooling in Western Europe: a Social History*. Albany: SUNY, 1985.

McManus, Antonia. *The Irish Hedge School and its Books*. Dublin: Four Courts Press, 2004.

Millar, Anne. 'Education during the Second World War.' www.wartimecanada.ca/essay/learning/education-during-second-world-war Accessed 4 November 2015.

Montessori, Maria. *The Montessori Method* (English edition, 1912).

Murphy, Ann and D. Raftery. *Emily Davies 1861–1875: Collected Letters*. USA: University of Virginia Press, 2002.

Paietta, Ann C. *Teachers in the Movies: A Filmography*. USA and UK: McFarland & Co., 2007.

Pearsall, Ronald. *Night's Black Angels: The Forms and Faces of Victorian Cruelty*. London: 1975.

Parkes, Susan. *Kildare Place: The History of the Church of Ireland Training College and College of Education 1811–2010*. Dublin: CICE. 2011.

Raftery, Deirdre. "Teaching as a profession for first-generation women graduates: a comparison of sources from Ireland, England and North America." *Irish Educational Studies*, Vol. 16, 1997.

Raftery, Deirdre. *Women and Learning in English Writing, 1600–1900*. Dublin: Four Courts Press, 1996.

Raftery, Deirdre. "Home Education in Nineteenth Century Ireland: The Role and Status of the Governess." *Irish Educational Studies* 19, no. 1 (2000): 308–17.

Raftery, Deirdre. "The Academic Formation of the Fin De Siecle Female: Schooling for Girls in Late Nineteenth Century Ireland." *Irish Educational Studies* 20, no. 1 (2001): 321–34.

Raftery, Deirdre and Susan Parkes. *Female Education in Ireland, 1700–1900: Minerva or Madonna?* Dublin and Portland, Oregon: I.A.P. 2007.

Raftery, Deirdre, Jane McDermid, and Gareth Elwyn Jones. "Social Change and Education in Ireland, Scotland and Wales: Historiography on Nineteenth-Century Schooling." *History of Education* 36, no. 4–5 (2007): 447–63.

Raftery, Deirdre, and Catherine Nowlan Roebuck. "Convent Schools and National Education in Nineteenth-Century Ireland: Negotiating a Place within a Nondenominational System." *History of Education* 36, no. 3 (2007): 353–65.

Raftery, Deirdre, Judith Harford, and Susan M. Parkes. "Mapping the Terrain of Female Education in Ireland, 1830–1910." *Gender and Education* 22, no. 5 (2010): 565–78.

Raftery, Deirdre. "Religions and the History of Education: A Historiography." *History of Education* 41, no. 1 (2012): 41–56.

Raftery, Deirdre. "The 'mission' of Nuns in Female Education in Ireland, c.1850–1950." *Paedagogica Historica* 48, no. 2 (2012): 299–313.

Raftery, Deirdre, and Karin Fischer (eds), *Educating Ireland: Schooling and Social Change, 1700–2000*. Dublin: Irish Academic Press, 2014.

Rusk, Robert. *Doctrines of the Great Educators*. London: Macmillan and Co., 1918.

Simon, Judith, and Linda Tuhiwai Smith (eds). *A Civilizing Mission? Perceptions and Representations of the New Zealand Native Schools System*. NZ: Auckland University Press, 2001.

Steinbach, Susie. *Women in England 1760–1914: A Social History*. Weidenfeld and Nicolson, 2003.

Strieb, Lynne. *A (Philadelphia) Teacher's Journal*. USA: University of North Dakota, 1985.

Tucker, G. Richard, and David Corson. *Encyclopedia of Language and Education*. Vol 4. Toronto: Springer, 1997.

Whittaker, David J. *The Impact and Legacy of Educational Sloyd: Head and Hands in Harness*. Oxon.: Routledge, 2014.

Yorke, Lois K. "Edwards, Anna Harriette," in *Dictionary of Canadian Biography*, vol. 14, University of Toronto/Université Laval, 2003. www.biographi.ca/en/bio/edwards_anna_harriette_14E.html Accessed 19 January 2015.

ADDITIONAL READING LIST
Select novels on the theme of teaching and education, 1916–2006

James Joyce, *Portrait of the Artist as a Young Man* (1916).
Antonia White, *Frost in May* (1933).
James Hilton, *Goodbye, Mr. Chips* (1934).
Dorothy L. Sayers, *Gaudy Night* (1935).
Kate O'Brien, *The Land of Spices* (1941).
Evelyn Waugh, *Brideshead Revisited* (1945).
Mary McCarthy, *The Groves of Academe* (1951).
Evan Hunter, *The Blackboard Jungle* (1954).
Kingsley Amis, *Lucky Jim* (1954).
John Knowles, *A Separate Peace* (1959).
Muriel Spark, *The Prime of Miss Jean Brodie* (1961).
Bel Kaufman, *Up the Down Staircase* (1964).
John Williams, *Stoner* (1965).
Joan Lindsay, *Picnic at Hanging Rock* (1967).
Tom Sharpe, *Porterhouse Blue* (1974).
Tobias Wolff, *Old School* (2003).
Zoë Heller, *Notes on a Scandal* (2003).
Zadie Smith, *On Beauty* (2005).
Frank McCourt, *Teacher Man* (2005).
Ian McEwan, *Solar* (2006).

FILMOGRAPHY
Films on the theme of teaching and education, 1920–2006

Schoolmaster Matsumoto (1920)
School of Life (1949)
Blackboard Jungle (1955)
The Miracle Worker (1962)
To Sir, with Love (1965)
The Prime of Miss Jean Brodie (1969)
Conrack (1974)
Fame (1980)
Teachers (1984)
Children of a Lesser God (1986)
Stand and Deliver (1988)
Lean on Me (1989)
Dead Poets Society (1989)
Sister Act (1992)
Sister Act 2: Back in the Habit (1993)
Renaissance Man (1994)
Dangerous Minds (1995)
Music of the Heart (1999)
The Chorus (2004)
Take the Lead (2006)

Addresses and websites

ORGANIZATIONS
North Bennet Street School
One of the early exponents of Sloyd education (see page 102) in the United States, North Bennet Street School (NBSS) offers intensive, hands-on training in traditional trades and fine craftsmanship, helping students to achieve meaningful lives and livelihoods. For more than a century, the exceptional programs, master faculty, and inspiring community have encouraged individual growth, curiosity, technical mastery, and commitment to excellence.
150 North Street
Boston MA 02109
www.nbss.edu

Teach for America
The mission is to enlist, develop, and mobilize as many as possible of our nation's most promising future leaders to grow and strengthen the movement for educational equity and excellence (see pages 162–165).
www.teachforamerica.org

Poetry Out Loud
The National Endowment for the Arts and the Poetry Foundation have partnered with U.S. state arts agencies to support Poetry Out Loud, a contest that encourages the nation's youth to learn about great poetry through memorization and recitation. This program helps students master public speaking skills, build self-confidence, and learn about their literary heritage.
www.poetryoutloud.org

World Teachers' Day
World Teachers' Day (WTD) held annually on October 5 is a UNESCO initiative, a day devoted to appreciating, assessing, and improving the educators of the world. WTD is a natural extension of UNESCO's year-round work of promoting teachers, ensuring that this profession, so vital to the healthy functioning of society, is itself "healthy."
www.worldteachersday.org

National Teacher of the Year
The National Teacher of the Year (NTOY) Program began in 1952 and continues as the oldest, most prestigious national honors program that focuses public attention on excellence in teaching.
www.ccsso.org/ntoy.html

TEACHING MUSEUMS
CALIFORNIA
Museum of Teaching and Learning, California
1111 E. Commonwealth, Unit C, Fullerton, CA 92831
www.motal.org

The Children's Creativity Museum
221 Fourth St., San Francisco, CA 94103
www. creativity.org

ILLINOIS
Bronzeville Children's Museum
9301 S. Stony Island Avenue, Chicago, IL 60617
www.bronzevillechildrensmuseum.com

Chicago Children's Museum
700 E. Grand Avenue, Chicago, IL 60611
www.chicagochildrensmuseum.org

Kohl Children's Museum
2100 Patriot Boulevard, Glenview, IL 60026
www.kohlchildrensmuseum.org

MASSACHUSETTS
Boston Children's Museum
308 Congress St., Boston, MA 02210
www.bostonchildrensmuseum.org

NEVADA
Discovery Children's Museum
360 Promenade Place, Las Vegas, NV 89106
www.discoverykidslv.org

NEW HAMPSHIRE
The Museum of Childhood, New Hampshire
2784 Wakefield Road, Wakefield, NH 03872
www.childrens-museum.org

NEW YORK
Brooklyn Children's Museum
145 Brooklyn Avenue, Brooklyn, NY 11213
www.brooklynkids.org

Children's Center at 42nd Street
Ground Floor, Room 84, New York Public Library, New York, NY 10026
www.nypl.org/about/locations/ schwarzman/childrens-center-42nd-street

Long Island Children's Museum
11 Davis Avenue,
Garden City, NY 11530
www.licm.org

OHIO
**The Children's Museum of
Cleveland**
10730 Euclid Avenue,
Cleveland, OH 44106
www.clevelandchildrensmuseum.org

PENNSYLVANIA
Please Touch Museum
4231 Avenue of the Republic,
Philadelphia, PA 19131
www.pleasetouchmuseum.org

**Education Division, Philadelphia
Museum of Art**
2600 Benjamin Franklin Parkway,
Philadelphia, PA 19130
educate@philamuseum.org

SOUTH CAROLINA
**The Museum of Education, South
Carolina**
Wardlaw Hall,
University of South Carolina,
Columbia, SC 29208
museumofeducation@sc.edu

TEXAS
The Children's Museum of Houston
1500 Binz,
Houston, Texas 77004
www.cmhouston.org

CANADA
Canadian Children's Museum
Canadian Museum of History,
100 Laurier Street,
Gatineau, Quebec K1A 0M8
www.historymuseum.ca/childrens-
museum

**ONE-ROOM SCHOOLHOUSE
MUSEUMS**
There are examples of one-room
schoolhouses all over North
America. A list can be found on:
oneroomschoolhousecenter.weebly.com

**TEACHING MUSEUMS AND
RESOURCE CENTERS**
**Blackwell History of Education
Museum**
The Learning Center,
Northern Illinois University,
DeKalb, IL 60115
www.cedu.niu.edu/blackwell

Museum of Teaching & Learning
1925 Skyline Drive,
Fullerton, CA 92831
www.motal.org

**Teacher Partner Program: Museum
of Science, Boston**
1 Science Park,
Boston, MA 02114
www.mos.org/teacher-partners

**Teacher Resource Center, Queen's
University Library**
Duncan McArthur Hall,
Queen's University,
Kingston, Ontario K7M 5R7
http://library.queensu.ca/webtrc

Holocaust Teacher Resource Center
Holocaust Education Foundation, Inc.,
P.O. Box 6153,
Newport News, VA 23606-6153
www.holocaust-trc.org

Smithsonian Museum
10th St. & Constitution Avenue NW,
Washington, D.C. 20560
www.si.edu

**Russell B. Nye Popular Culture
Collection**
Special Collections,
Main Library Building,
Michigan State University,
366 W. Circle Drive,
East Lansing MI, 48824
www.lib.msu.edu/spc/collections/nye

Index

Picture Credits

The publisher would like to thank the following sources for their permission to reproduce the photographs and illustrations in this book:

Acknowledgments

AUTHOR'S ACKNOWLEDGMENTS

The following are acknowledged with gratitude: IBVM International Archives, Dublin; Oberlin College Archives; RSCJ Archives, Roehampton; Queen's College London Archives; Mary Evans Picture Library; the National Gallery of Ireland; the Museum of London; Teach For America; the Boston Clemente Program; Dr. Wanda Gregory; Professor Ann B. Murphy; Mary Joy Langdon IJS; Fiona Loughnane.

The work of three oral historians who have gathered the voices of teachers in the United States and New Zealand is especially acknowledged: Arlene Alda, Anne Else, and Luther Bryan Clegg.

Finally, my thanks to publisher Judith More, and to picture editor Emily Hedges.

FIL ROUGE PRESS ACKNOWLEDGMENTS

Deirdre Raftery for her enthusiasm and hard work, and all at Barron's Educational Series for their belief in and support for the book.

The team at Fil Rouge Press would also like to acknowledge teachers who have particularly inspired them:

Judith More would like to thank her parents and first teachers; art teacher Audrey More and geography teacher and headmaster Peter More; her French teacher at Oxford High School, Mrs. Balhatchet, and her English and drama teacher at Lord Williams School, Gerard Gould.

Janis Utton would like to thank Mick Sparksman, her Graphics Lecturer at Lowestoft School of Art.

Emily Hedges would like to thank her English teacher, Mrs. White, who brought Shakespeare alive, and her friend from university, Inga Bryden, who is now an inspiring teacher herself.

Thank you!